THE ADVENTURE TRAVELERS GUIDE

The 50 State Travel Challenge

By

Mikjeala Thomas

9 780578 853970

DEDICATED TO

My family and friends who motivated me when I felt
disconnected, who supported me when I didn't know I needed it,
and who have believed in every adventure that I set out to
explore.

Thank you!

TABLE OF CONTENTS

ABOUT THIS TRAVEL GUIDE

This travel guide was created for the travelers who desire to make the most out of every vacation. It is especially helpful for those who find it challenging to plan activities or just don't have the time to commit to the planning process. The interactive nature of this guide is uniquely designed not just to offer recommendations to help enhance your vacation plans but also to create some spontaneous fun along the way!

Here, we will break down the best things to do in all 50 states in the United States of America. There are three categories for each state: Activities, Food & Drinks, and Culture & More Adventure. Each category has three challenge levels to choose from: Challenge #1 is the most economical choice and modest activity level, Challenge #2 offers a comfortable medium for both, and Challenge #3, which is for those seeking the most extreme adventures and may require more of a financial commitment.

For each state you will find the top cities to visit, the best time to go, hidden gems, bucket list items, fun festivals each state is known for, and for the 21 and up crowd it even offers signature adult beverages that may be fun to try in their state of origin!

HOW TO USE THIS TRAVEL GUIDE

For each state, there are three sections: Activities, Food & Drinks, and Culture & More Adventure.

Above each category box you will find an estimated price range for the activities. This will help give you an idea of activity costs prior to your vacation to help with budgeting. The beautiful thing about this guide is that there are activities to fit every budget—you don't have to break the bank to create a fun experience!

It is recommended that you scratch off or mark your desired challenges prior to going on your trip.
This will not only help with budgeting, but it will prepare you just in case advance reservations for activities or restaurants are required.

It is also important to remember the structure of the challenges and the order in which they are ranked to help you decide which challenge(s) you would like to scratch off or complete first. Of course, if you are feeling extremely adventurous, you can scratch off all the challenges and complete all the tasks on your vacation!

CHALLENGE KEY

Challenge Level 1 – Beginner - $
Challenge Level 2 – Intermediate - $$
Challenge Level 3 – Expert - $$$

Don't forget that this book is a keepsake! Begin your journey of completing the 50-state challenge and be sure to take pictures with your polaroid camera (or just actually print out the pictures taken on your phone or DSLR camera). Save and post the pictures in the open space next to the challenge box and share the memories with loved ones.

Let the adventure begin!

Disclaimer: Some activities may require a car. Prices for activities are estimates and are subject to change. Quoted prices are per person.

Deluxe Version Only: *Scratch off directions only apply to the deluxe version of this book.*

The top cities to visit are listed for every state. Some activities are city specific.

ALABAMA

TOP CITIES: Montgomery, Birmingham, Mobile, Huntsville, Gulf Shores
BEST TIME TO TRAVEL: Summer (June), Fall (September-November)
SIGNATURE DRINK: Yellow Hammer (vodka, Malibu rum, pineapple juice, orange juice)
HIDDEN GEMS: Visit the unclaimed baggage center, Spear hunting museum
BUCKET LIST: Turtle nesting season (5/1-8/31), Battleship USS Alabama, Visit Cherokee Rock Village and climb giant boulders
FESTIVALS: Mobile Mardi Gras, National Shrimp Festival in Gulf Shores, Sidewalk Film Festival

---

$Costs range from $18-$100

<u>Activities</u>

$ Challenge #1

➢ Spend the day at Dismals Canyon hiking and observing the canyon's waterfalls and nature. Then take a night tour to see the bioluminescent worms and caves glow!

$$ Challenge #2

➢ Tackle the treetop obstacle course and the ziplining at Red Mountain Park.

$$$ Challenge #3

➢ Grab your camera and go caving in Neversink Pit in Fackler, Alabama (permit required).

PLACE PICTURE HERE

ALABAMA

Food & Drinks

$ Challenge #1

> Ask a local to recommend the best locally owned restaurant. A must is to try what Alabama is known for... fried green tomatoes, lane cake, and pecan pie! Wash it down with the native Yellow Hammer drink.

$$ Challenge #2

> Skip the traditional restaurant and eat in a cave! Visit "The Cave Restaurant", also known as Rattlesnake Saloon.

$$$ Challenge #3

> Visit the Battleship Parkway between Mobile and Spanish Fort. Hop from restaurant to restaurant with friends and family and eat family style to try all of the best seafood dishes.

PLACE PICTURE HERE

PLACE PICTURE HERE

$Costs range from $10-$60

Culture & More Adventure

$ Challenge #1

> Time for some culture! Visit as many museums as you can: Montgomery Museum of Art, Birmingham Museum of Art, Legacy Museum, and the Birmingham Civil Rights Institute.

$$ Challenge #2

> Visit The Wharf in Gulf Shores! It has premium outlets, entertainment, and great food. There is something to do for everyone.

$$$ Challenge #3

> It's tiki time! Spend the day on a floating tiki hut and cruise the shores of Orange Beach while sipping a refreshing cocktail.

ALASKA

TOP CITIES: Anchorage, Fairbanks, Juneau, Ketchikan
BEST TIME TO TRAVEL: Summer (May–September), Winter (October, November, April)
SIGNATURE DRINKS: Duck Farts (Kahlua, Baileys Irish Cream, whiskey), Smoked Salmon Vodka Bloody Mary (Smoked Salmon Vodka, V8, Tabasco, Worcestershire sauce, sugar, salt, ground black pepper, celery)
HIDDEN GEMS: Ice Glacier Margaritas, Alaska Chilkat Bald Eagle Preserve, Take a float plane to Cook Inlet and see beluga whales, Salmon spawning, Pribilof Islands, Wrangell-St. Elias National Park and Preserve, Wood-Tikchik State Park, Spirit House
BUCKET LIST: See the Alaskan northern lights, Tongass National Park to view the Pack Creek brown bears, Tracy Arm Fjord, Hop on a jetboat and cruise the Talkeetna to spot wildlife, Take an air safari bush plane adventure, Mendenhall Glacier helicopter tours, Take a boat ride to get up close and personal with seals, whales, and other sea life
FESTIVALS: Alaska State Fair, Fur Rendezvous Festival, Anchorage Market

$Costs range from $15-$300

Activities

$ Challenge #1

➢ Spot the Alaskan big five! Visit Denali National Park and try to take a picture of yourself with one of these five animals in the background: moose, bear, caribou, Dall sheep, wolf.

$$ Challenge #2

➢ All aboard! Hop on the Alaska Railroad and travel from city to city. Take a selfie on the train with a scenic background.

$$$ Challenge #3

➢ Do a dog sledding/mushing tour.

PLACE PICTURE HERE

ALASKA

Food & Drinks

$ Challenge #1

➢ Ask a local for the best restaurant to have Alaskan king crab and a Duck Fart.

$$ Challenge #2

➢ Try some of Alaska's local iconic food: reindeer dogs, black cod, Akutaq/Eskimo ice cream, muktuk, smoked salmon, and other locally sourced seafood.

$$$ Challenge #3

➢ Create your own food tour and eat at as many locally owned restaurants as you can find. Allow a local to choose your dish at each location (for detailed guides, visit www.TheTravelBella.com).

PLACE PICTURE HERE

PLACE PICTURE HERE

$Costs range from $125-$200

Culture & More Adventure

$ Challenge #1

➢ Go kayaking on the Inside Passage in Haines.

$$ Challenge #2

➢ Take a dip in Chena Hot Springs while watching the northern lights.

$$$ Challenge #3

➢ Go whale watching in Juneau and visit the Mendenhall Glacier.

ARIZONA

TOP CITIES: Phoenix, Scottsdale, Sedona, Tucson
BEST TIME TO TRAVEL: Spring (March–May), Winter (December–February)
SIGNATURE DRINKS: Prickly Pear Margaritas, Tequila Sunrise
HIDDEN GEMS: Any spiritual retreats in Sedona, Paria Canyon, Buckskin Gulch, Wrather Arch, Titan Missile Museum, Arcosanti, Canyon De Chelly National Monument, Mojave Desert
BUCKET LIST: The Wave - a psychedelic rock formation in Vermillion Cliffs National Monument, The Painted Desert, Rafting or riding a mule through the Grand Canyon, Take a nighttime moon hike through Boynton Canyon to witness the Milky Way galaxy
FESTIVALS: Taco Festival, Street Eats Food Truck Festival, Summer Ends Music Festival

$Costs range from $15-$165

Activities

$ Challenge #1

> Visit the Oak Street Alley Murals in Phoenix and take pictures to remember in front of the various street art.

$$ Challenge #2

> Take a day trip to the Grand Canyon and swim in Havasupai Falls.

$$$ Challenge #3

> Hop in the car and drive to Antelope Canyon for canoeing or hiking.

PLACE PICTURE HERE

ARIZONA

Food & Drinks

$ Challenge #1

➢ Visit the famous Little Miss BBQ. Afterwards, find a bar that serves the best Prickly Pear Margaritas.

$$ Challenge #2

➢ Try some of the local flavors of Arizona. Ask a local for the best places to try Sonoran hot dogs, dates, chimichangas, Navajo tacos, posole, and tamales.

$$$ Challenge #3

➢ Do a treasure hunt to find and taste the best food truck spots around Arizona.

PLACE PICTURE HERE

PLACE PICTURE HERE

$Costs range from $25-$125

Culture & More Adventure

$ Challenge #1

➢ Experience the Desert Botanical Garden during the day, and then go wine tasting on the Verde Valley Wine Trail.

$$ Challenge #2

➢ Hop on a party bike and do a guided city tour, enjoying some drinks as you pedal.

$$$ Challenge #3

➢ Go to Lake Powell and do various water activites like wakeboarding, ski tubing, water skiing, and kneeboarding.

ARKANSAS

TOP CITIES: Little Rock, Hot Springs, Fayetteville, Eureka Springs
BEST TIME TO TRAVEL: Spring (April-May), Fall (October – November)
SIGNATURE DRINKS: Whiskey Sprite, Cynthiana wine, Arkansas Razorback (vodka, rum, amaretto liqueur, Kahlua)
HIDDEN GEMS: Garvan Woodland Gardens (Hot Springs), Crystal Bridges Museum of American Art, Mount Magazine State Park, Ozark Medieval Fortress
BUCKET LIST: Mildred B Cooper Memorial Chapel, Crystal Bridges Museum of American Art
FESTIVALS: Watermelon Festival, Lights of the Ozarks, RiverFest

---

$Costs range from $10-$125

Activities

$ Challenge #1

➢ Take a float on the Buffalo River in a canoe, kayak or raft.

$$ Challenge #2

➢ Diamonds are everyone's best friend! Dig for diamonds at Crater of Diamonds State Park. Remember, it's finders' keepers!

$$$ Challenge #3

➢ Visit a natural hot spring outside or a traditional bath house and relax in the thermal mineral waters. (Visit www.TheTravelBella.com for an inclusive list of the various hot springs in the United States.

PLACE PICTURE HERE

ARKANSAS

$Costs range from $15-$35

Food & Drinks

$ Challenge #1

➤ Enjoy a local treat and eat at the historical Ray's Rump Shack.

$$ Challenge #2

➤ Do a food scavenger hunt to try some local treats: potato doughnuts, Arkansas Black apples, snow cream, Southern butter rolls, possum pie, and buffalo ribs.

$$$ Challenge #3

➤ Find a local dive bar for drinks and meet new quirky personalities. Order a renown Arkansas Whiskey & Sprite.

PLACE PICTURE HERE

$Costs range from $10-$85

Culture & More Adventure

$ Challenge #1

➤ It's culture time! Visit as many museums as you can: Arkansas Art Center, Museum of Discovery, Crystal Bridges Museum of American Art, Children's Museum, The Walmart Museum.

$$ Challenge #2

➤ Step off the beaten path and take a ride on the Arkansas & Missouri Railroad.

$$$ Challenge #3

➤ Hike Whitaker Point and have someone take an Instaworthy picture of you from a distance at the edge of the cliff!

PLACE PICTURE HERE

CALIFORNIA

TOP CITIES: Los Angeles, San Francisco, San Diego, San Jose, Oakland, Napa, Newport Beach, Palm Springs, Sacramento

BEST TIME TO TRAVEL: Year round

SIGNATURE DRINK: Red wine

HIDDEN GEMS: Glass Beach, Fort Bragg, Mammoth Lakes Hot Springs, Badwater Basin, Black Sands Beach in Sausalito, Highway 99, Death Valley sunsets & moving rocks, Hammock camping in Yosemite National Park's El Capitan, Ride the Powell-Hyde cable car in San Francisco, Bombay Beach, Lake Berryessa Spillway & Monticello Dam

BUCKET LIST: Hike Yosemite Point for the best views and to climb the Half Dome cables (permit required), Walk or bike across the Golden Gate Bridge, Wine tasting in Napa Valley, Alcatraz Island, Hollywood Walk of Fame, Venice Beach, Lombard St. in San Francisco, Gold panning in Jamestown

FESTIVALS: Coachella, Stagecoach, BottleRock Napa Valley, Lightning in a Bottle, various film festivals, Fresno Fair

$Costs range from $5-$85

<u>Activities</u>

$ Challenge #1

➤ Go stargazing at Glacier Point in Yosemite.

$$ Challenge #2

➤ Instaworthy! Visit the following locations and take some creative, fun pictures: Secret Tiled Staircase, The Last Bookstore, and Glass Beach.

$$$ Challenge #3

➤ Rent a car for the day and take a drive along the coastline of Big Sur. Don't forget to park and take some time to explore and hike Big Sur!

PLACE PICTURE HERE

CALIFORNIA

$Costs range from $12-$40

Food & Drinks

$ Challenge #1

➤ Take a day trip to the Mosaic Tile House. Afterwards, do the ultimate treasure hunt and try to find the best speakeasy bar in the area.

$$ Challenge #2

➤ Every day is Taco Tuesday! Take a taco tour and eat some of the best authentic tacos that California has to offer.

$$$ Challenge #3

➤ Support the local business owners! Research and indulge in the endless options for various independently owned restaurants or food trucks.

PLACE PICTURE HERE

PLACE PICTURE HERE

$Costs range from $10-$125

Culture & More Adventure

$ Challenge #1

➤ Go shopping at one of Cali's open-air markets: Grand Central Market, The Original Farmers Market, Hollywood Farmers' Market, Hollywood Night Market, Melrose Trading Post, Downtown LA Farmers Market, Ferry Building Market, or The Grove.

$$ Challenge #2 – San Francisco

➤ Visit the Cable Car Museum. Hop on the cable car and take a picture of yourself hanging off it!

$$$ Challenge #3

➤ Go kayaking or rent a motor boat in June Lake Loop.

COLORADO

TOP CITIES: Denver, Vail, Colorado Springs, Aspen, Steamboat Springs, Telluride
BEST TIME TO TRAVEL: Year round (Winter for snow activities)
SIGNATURE DRINKS: Craft beer, The Tree Line (cherries, whiskey, herbal liqueur, lemon juice, simple syrup), Colorado Bulldog (vodka, coffee liqueur, light cream, cola)
HIDDEN GEMS: Bishop Castle in San Isabel National Forest, Mesa Verde Balcony House, Garden of the Gods, San Juan Skyway and the Durango & Silverton Narrow Gauge Railroad, Red Feather Lakes, Shambhala Mountain Center
BUCKET LIST: Skiing in Aspen, Telluride or Colorado Springs, Telluride Mountain Village Gondola, Explore the Western Slopes in Palisade, Grand Junction and Fruita, Whitewater rafting on the Colorado River, Cliff Palace, Cycle the Leadville Trail, Climb the long, steep ladders into Mesa Verde's Balcony House, Visit Grand Lake
FESTIVALS: Sonic Bloom Festival, Arise Music Festival, Hanuman Festival, The Ride Festival, Global Dance Festival, Colorado Artfest

$Costs range from $20-$200

Activities

$ Challenge #1

- ➤ Take a day trip to soak in the Desert Reef Hot Springs or visit another luxury hot springs location.

$$ Challenge #2

- ➤ Escape the daily hustle of the city and visit Sand Dunes National Park for some sandboarding sand sledding!

$$$ Challenge #3

- ➤ Go skiing or take a snowmobile tour.

PLACE PICTURE HERE

COLORADO

$Costs range from $15-$40

Food & Drinks

$ Challenge #1

➤ Visit Linger Eatery or Avanti Food & Beverage for a wide array of food options.

$$ Challenge #2

➤ Partake in a beer, whiskey, or wine tasting.

$$$ Challenge #3

➤ Eat like a local and try the following local food favorites: Mexican hamburger, Fool's Gold Loaf, Superman ice cream, Rocky Mountain oysters, bison, and Indian/ Navajo tacos.

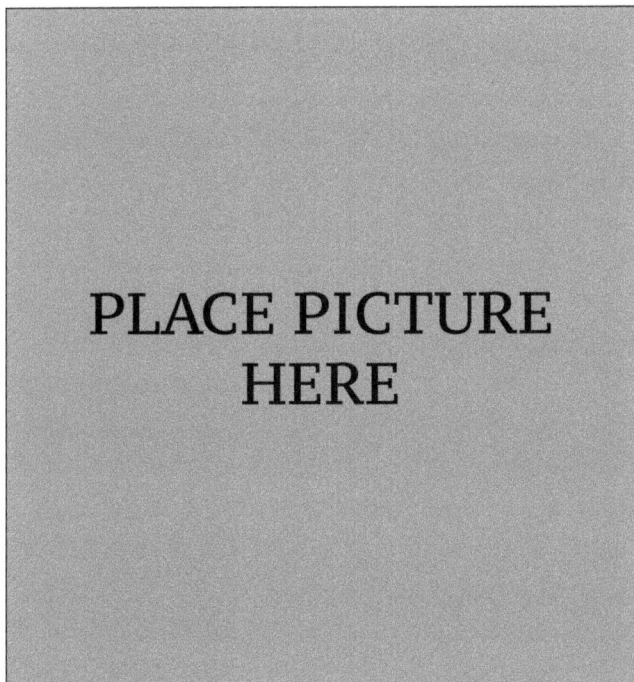

PLACE PICTURE HERE

PLACE PICTURE HERE

$Costs range from $20-$160

Culture & More Adventure

$ Challenge #1

➤ For the love of art! Go on a Denver street art tour and visit the River North Art District to feel inspired.

$$ Challenge #2

➤ Instaworthy! Grab the camera and take a trip to the Maroon Bells mountains near Aspen.

$$$ Challenge #3

➤ Grab some axes and go ice climbing on a frozen waterfall. Afterwards find a natural hot spring and relax.

CONNECTICUT

TOP CITIES: Hartford, New Haven, Bridgeport, Stamford, Manchester, Waterbury, Kent, Stonington

BEST TIME TO TRAVEL: Spring (May-June), Fall (September-October)

SIGNATURE DRINKS: White wine, Moscow Mule (vodka, ginger beer, fresh lime), Dark 'n Stormy (dark rum, ginger beer, lime juice)

HIDDEN GEMS: Cathedral Pines Preserve in Cornwall, Holy Land in Waterbury, Saville Dam in Barkhamsted, Visit Stars Hollow - the town that inspired the show Gilmore Girls, Sherlock Holmes Castle at Gillette Castle State Park, Thimble Islands

BUCKET LIST: Visit the State Capitol building, Explore the Mark Twain House & Museum, Climb or hike in Bluff Point State Park, Visit the Yale University Art Gallery, In the winter months hike in snowshoes through the forest and meadows

FESTIVALS: Apple Festival, Renaissance Faire, Greater Hartford Festival of Jazz

$Costs range from $0-$75
Activities

$ Challenge #1

> Instaworthy! Grab the camara and visit the Elizabeth Park Rose Garden.

$$ Challenge #2

> Go camping in Hammonasset Beach State Park and indulge in the beach life.

$$$ Challenge #3

> Take the Highflyer Zipline over the Foxwoods Resort Casino.

PLACE PICTURE HERE

CONNECTICUT

$Costs range from $10-$150

Food & Drinks

$ Challenge #1

➢ Connecticut is known for its unique culinary experiences. Find a local farm-to- fork dining experience and enjoy. Visit www.TheTravelBella.com for recommendations.

$$ Challenge #2

➢ Visit Haight-Brown Vineyard for wine, cheese, and chocolate tastings.

$$$ Challenge #3

➢ Take a journey along the Connecticut Wine Trail. Find your favorite bottle of wine and take it home as a souvenir.

PLACE PICTURE HERE

PLACE PICTURE HERE

$Costs range from $10-$100

Culture & More Adventure

$ Challenge #1

➢ Visit the Aldrich Contemporary Art Museum.

$$ Challenge #2

➢ Experience the one-of-a-kind magnificent outdoor murals, be inspired, and take some colorful pictures.

$$$ Challenge #3

➢ Climb aboard the Essex Steam Train & River Boat and take in some scenic views to remember.

DELAWARE

TOP CITIES: New Castle, Wilmington, Dover, Rehoboth Beach, Newark, Dewey Beach, Delaware City

BEST TIME TO TRAVEL: Summer (June–August)

SIGNATURE DRINKS: Dogfish Head, Orange Crush (orange vodka, triple sec, Sprite or soda water, orange juice)

HIDDEN GEMS: Trap Pond State Park, Air Mobility Command Museum, Johnson Victoria Museum

BUCKET LIST: Ryves Holt House, duPont's Art & Antiques at Nemours Estate

FESTIVALS: Mount Center Wildflower Celebration, NASCAR Races, Delaware State Fair, Sea Witch Festival

---

$Costs range from $25-$75

Activities

$ Challenge #1

➤ Go rock climbing at Alapocas Run State Park.

$$ Challenge #2

➤ Feeling adventurous? Take windsurfing lessons in Rehoboth Bay or a boat ride on the Lewes Rehoboth Canal.

$$$ Challenge #3

➤ Kayak on the Delaware Bradywine River.

PLACE PICTURE HERE

DELAWARE

Food & Drinks

$ Challenge #1

➤ Take a tour of the Dogfish Head Brewery to taste some local beer.

$$ Challenge #2

➤ Visit a local orchard to handpick your own fruit.

$$$ Challenge #3

➤ Try out the tiki bar or eat on the waterfront at Harpoon Hannah's in Fenwick Island, or find a good rooftop resturant to eat at while taking in the city views.

PLACE PICTURE HERE

PLACE PICTURE HERE

$Costs range from $4-$35

Culture & More Adventure

$ Challenge #1

➤ Experience horseshoe crab spawning on Bay Beach.

$$ Challenge #2

➤ Watch a movie on the beach in the summer at Dewey Beach.

$$$ Challenge #3

➤ Go birding at Bombay Hook National Wildlife Refuge.

FLORIDA

TOP CITIES: Orlando, Miami, Panama City Beach, Destin, Tampa, Jacksonville, Tallahassee, Fort Lauderdale

BEST TIME TO TRAVEL: Spring (February-May)

SIGNATURE DRINKS: Mimosa, Mojito (white rum, fresh lime juice, mint leaves, sugar, soda water), Rum Runner (pineapple juice, orange juice, blackberry liqueur, banana liqueur, light rum, dark rum, grenadine)

HIDDEN GEMS: Payne's Prairie Preserve, The Holy Land Experience, Club E11even (24-hour multi-level club), Biscayne National Park, Mallory Square in Keywest, Stiltsville, Ah-Tah-Thi-Ki Museum

BUCKET LIST: Drink Butterbeer at the Wizarding World of Harry Potter, Experience marine life at Dry Tortugas National Park, See live mermaids at Weeki Wachee Springs State Park, Take an airboat ride through the Everglades, Go snorkeling through a rainbow reef

FESTIVALS: Art Basel, Art Deco Weekend, Everglades Seafood Festival, Coconut Grove Arts Festival, Shark Tooth Festival, SunFest, Octoberfest

---

$Costs range from $25-$250

Activities

$ Challenge #1

➤ Snorkel in the Devil's Den or go scuba diving at Neptune Memorial Reef.

$$ Challenge #2

➤ Take a bioluminescence night kayak tour or swim with manatees at Crystal River.

$$$ Challenge #3

➤ Spend the night glamping in the Everglades in a chickee hut.

PLACE PICTURE HERE

FLORIDA

$Costs range from $15-$90

Food & Drinks

$ Challenge #1

➢ Catch a murder mystery dinner train in Fort Myers.

$$ Challenge #2

➢ Go on a scavenger hunt and try some local favorites: Key lime pie, Florida stone crab, conch fritters, Cuban sandwich, Apalachicola oysters, strawberry shortcake, gator tail, gator bites, smoked fish.

$$$ Challenge #3

➢ Take an authentic Little Havana food and culture tour. Don't forget to try a renown Florida Mojito.

PLACE PICTURE HERE

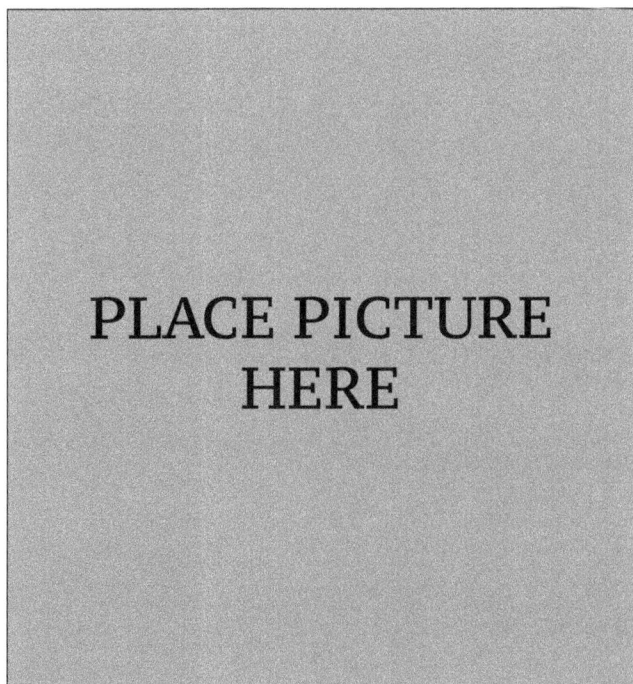

PLACE PICTURE HERE

$Costs range from $89-$300

Culture & More Adventure

$ Challenge #1

➢ Charter a boat and go deep sea fishing in the Gulf of Mexico.

$$ Challenge #2

➢ Ride an airboat through Sawgrass Recreation Park and hold a baby alligator.

$$$ Challenge #3

➢ Take kitesurfing lessons in Miami on the beach.

GEORGIA

TOP CITIES: Atlanta, Savannah, Buckhead, Little Five Points, Midtown, Stone Mountain
BEST TIME TO TRAVEL: Year round
SIGNATURE DRINKS: Scarlet O'Hara (Southern Comfort, cranberry juice, lime juice), The Georgia Peach (Peach Schnapps, Vodka, Orange Juice, Grenadine, Southern Comfort)
HIDDEN GEMS: Tallulah Falls, Ponce City Market, Historic Old Fourth Ward, Highland Avenue for bars and shops, Crypt of Civilization time capsule, Georgia Guidestones, Culture Experience interactive photo exhibit
BUCKET LIST: Visit the home of Martin Luther King Jr., Savannah Historic District, Climb Stone Mountain, go whitewater rafting on the Chattahoochee River
FESTIVALS: ONE Musicfest, Shaky Boots Music Festival, SweetWater 420 Festival, Food-O-Rama Food Truck Festival, Dogwood Festival

---

$Costs range from $20-$100

Activities

$ Challenge #1

> Ride electronic scooters and take creative pictures of yourself in front of the graffiti walls in the Krog Street Tunnel and visit the Atlanta Beltline.

$$ Challenge #2

> Stop in at the Atlanta Botanical Garden and go picture crazy!

$$$ Challenge #3

> Take a break from the chaos of city life and take a day trip to hike in Amicalola Falls State Park.

PLACE PICTURE HERE

GEORGIA

$Costs range from $5-$300

Food & Drinks

$ Challenge #1

➤ Its brunch time! Ask a local for the best rooftop brunch spot in Atlanta and go!

$$ Challenge #2

➤ Whether its Bourbon or Craft beer, pick your preference and visit the Old 4th Distillery for a tasting.

$$$ Challenge #3

➤ The best of the South! Do a southern food tour to sample the tastings of the best resturants in Atlanta. Try Georgia's signature drink, the Georgia Peach.

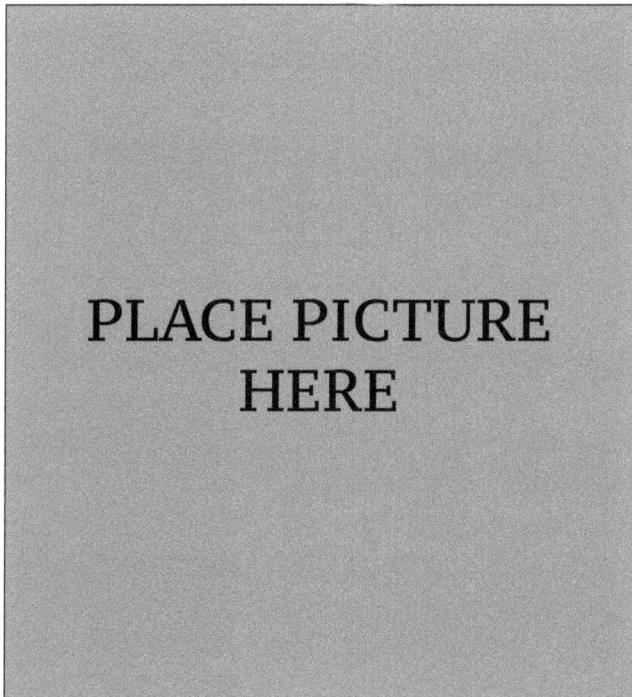

PLACE PICTURE HERE

PLACE PICTURE HERE

$Costs range from $15-$35

Culture & More Adventure

$ Challenge #1

➤ Explore Ponce City Market, and don't forget to go to the rooftop carnival for some childhood fun!

$$ Challenge #2

➤ Visit the National Center for Civil and Human Rights.

$$$ Challenge #3

➤ Instaworthy! Grab the camera and go to the Trap Music Museum for some photo ops and to learn some music history.

HAWAII

TOP CITIES: Honolulu, Hilo, Kailua-Kona, Hawi, Kailua, Kaneohe, Kapolei, Lahaina, Waianae, Waipahu, Lihu

BEST TIME TO TRAVEL: Year round (especially April, May, September, October)

SIGNATURE DRINKS: Green Bottles, Mai Tai (Koloa Gold Rum, Orange Curacao, orgeat-almond syrup, sugar cane juice, fresh lime juice, vanilla-infused simple syrup, dark rum floater)

HIDDEN GEMS: Byodo-In Temple, Punalu'u Black Sand Beach, Waipio Valley Black Sand Beach, Lumahai Beach, Hanauma Bay Nature Preserve, Pearl Harbor, Mauna Kea Observatories, Adak National Forest

BUCKET LIST: Hike the Puu Pehe Trail, Attend a Luau Feast, Visit Kauai's Glass Beach, Volcanoes National Park, Ride the waves and surf, Wander through a massive planet maze in Dole Plantations' giant Pineapple Garden, Jump the ultimate cliff at Pu'u Keka'a (Black Rock), Sleep on the beach and catch the sunrise, Go whale watching to see a Humpback whale

FESTIVALS: Aloha Festival, Waikiki Spam Jam, King Kamehameha Day, Made in Hawaii Festival

$Costs range from $25-$90

Activities

$ Challenge #1

> Climb the Stairway to Heaven at the Ha'iku Stairs of O'ahu.

$$ Challenge #2

> Hike or take a boat ride to the Na Pali Coast State Park to capture breathtaking views.

$$$ Challenge #3

> Go cliff jumping and swim in waterfalls at the Seven Sacred Pools.

PLACE PICTURE HERE

HAWAII

Food & Drinks

$ Challenge #1

> Eat like a local! Seek out the following Hawaiian foods and try them all: poi, laulau, kalua pig, lomi-lomi salmon, Hawaiian plate lunch, shaved ice cream, Taro Ko Farm chips, luau stew, strawberry mochi, coco puffs, cow pig bun burgers, croissada, manapua.

$$ Challenge #2

> Treat yourself to dinner on the beach and under the stars or on the water at Tidepools.

$$$ Challenge #3

> Take a cooking class to learn how to cook traditional Hawaiian food.

PLACE PICTURE HERE

PLACE PICTURE HERE

$Costs range from $69-$200

Culture & More Adventure

$ Challenge #1

> Stretch it out! For a night to remember, partake in an afterhours stand up paddle board yoga class at the beach.

$$ Challenge #2

> Pamper yourself with a traditional Balinese flower bath at Mandara Spa.

$$$ Challenge #3

> Go snorkeling with the turtles or diving with manta rays.

IDAHO

TOP CITIES: Boise, Idaho Falls, Meridian, Twin Falls
BEST TIME TO TRAVEL: Winter, Spring (March-May)
SIGNATURE DRINKS: Craft beer, Potato Vodka and Soda
HIDDEN GEMS: Box Canyon, Blue Heart Springs, Black Magic Canyon
BUCKET LIST: Tea Kettle Cave, Boise River Greenbelt, Oasis Bordello Museum, Museum of Clean, Hike the Sawtooth Range
FESTIVALS: Boise Music Festival, Teton Valley Balloon Rally, Idaho Mountain Festival

$Costs range from $25-$125

Activities

$ Challenge #1

➢ Chase waterfalls! Go paddle boarding or kayaking at the base of Shoshone Falls.

$$ Challenge #2

➢ Mountain bike through train tunnels and on high trestles on the Route of the Hiawatha.

$$$ Challenge #3

➢ Get your thrills with whitewater rafting in Hells Canyon or on the Salmon River.

PLACE PICTURE HERE

IDAHO

$Costs range from $45-$89

Food & Drinks

$ Challenge #1

➢ Eat like a local! Try the state's signature dishes: finger steaks, morel mushrooms, Key lime pie, huckleberry ice cream, trout, Ice Cream Potato, baked potato, bison burger, butter cake, Owyhee chocolates, and *don't forget* to try some huckleberry wine!

$$ Challenge #2

➢ A taste of Idaho! Do a food tour to taste the best of the best of Idaho.

$$$ Challenge #3

➢ Experience a one-of-a-kind winter dinner in Sun Valley.

PLACE PICTURE HERE

PLACE PICTURE HERE

$Costs range from $50-$299

Culture & More Adventure

$ Challenge #1

➢ Take a dip in one of several natural hot springs, sip some wine, and enjoy the views.

$$ Challenge #2

➢ Rent a scooter for the day and joy ride throughout the town as you shop and eat.

$$$ Challenge #3

➢ It's sleigh time! Choose between a sleigh ride or snowmobiling.

ILLINOIS

TOP CITIES: Chicago
BEST TIME TO TRAVEL: Spring (April-May), Fall (September-October)
SIGNATURE DRINKS: Bloody Mary with Chicago Absolut, Swedish Seed (Malört, Root Liqueur, lemon juice, brown sugar, honey syrup, bitters) JG&L (Jameson, ginger, lime)
HIDDEN GEMS: Starved Rock State Park
BUCKET LIST: Chicago Christmas Parade on Magnificent Mile
FESTIVALS: Taste of Chicago, Lollapalooza, Chicago Blues Festival, Grant Park Music Festival, Manifest

$Costs range from $15-$45

Activities

$ Challenge #1

➢ Be the ultimate tourist! Shop the Magnificent Mile, check out the Chicago Bean in Millennium Park, and live on the edge with the Willis Tower 1,353 ft Skydeck and glass boxes!

$$ Challenge #2

➢ Dive off the beaten path into Mermet Springs and check out the submerged airplane.

$$$ Challenge #3

➢ Rent a bicycle and enjoy a ride along Lake Shore Drive.

PLACE PICTURE HERE

ILLINOIS

$Costs range from $10-$45

Food & Drinks

$ Challenge #1

➢ Eat like a local! Local food favorites: deep dish pizza, Chicago style hot dogs, Home of the Hoagy, Garrett Popcorn, Italian beef dipped sandwich.

$$ Challenge #2

➢ Visit the French Market Chicago or the Time Out Market Chicago and choose from the many food vendors to try something new.

$$$ Challenge #3

➢ Take in the stunning views! Find a day party on a rooftop bar and enjoy some good drinks and food.

PLACE PICTURE HERE

PLACE PICTURE HERE

$Costs range from $40-$200

Culture & More Adventure

$ Challenge #1

➢ Take in the Chicago culture and experience one or all of the following: Art Institute of Chicago, river cruise architecture tour, or the Field Museum.

$$ Challenge #2

➢ Paddle board along the Chicago River, and afterwards, don't forget to check out the outdoor art gallery of the 16th Street murals.

$$$ Challenge #3

➢ Get a bird's eye view! Take a private helicopter ride to get the ultimate view of the Chicago skyline.

INDIANA

TOP CITIES: Indianapolis, Fort Wayne, South Bend, Gary
BEST TIME TO TRAVEL: Summer, Fall (September–October)
SIGNATURE DRINKS: Domestic beer or local Beer, Hoosier Heritage (apple cider, maple syrup, lemon juice)
HIDDEN GEMS: Amish Country
BUCKET LIST: Visit Pine Lake for some outdoor fun, the Children's Museum of Indianapolis, Haunted Indianapolis Ghost Walk
FESTIVALS: Indiana State Fair, Indianapolis Jazz in the Park, Greek Fest, St. Joan of Arc French Market

---

$Costs range from $5-$150

Activities

$ Challenge #1

➤ Capture the view of the city after climbing Monument Circle.

$$ Challenge #2

➤ Go fishing, swimming or boating at the Indiana Dunes National Lakeshore.

$$$ Challenge #3

➤ Have a little overnight fun at Bluespring Caverns, America's longest navigable underground river, and partake in a one of the many adventure packages.

PLACE PICTURE HERE

INDIANA

Food & Drinks

$ Challenge #1

> All aboard! Ride and dine on the themed Spirit of Jasper train.

$$ Challenge #2

> Drink and pedal! Hop on an Indy Pedal Pub, grab some drinks and tour the city.

$$$ Challenge #3

> Ask a local for restaurant recommendations. Feeling more adventurous? Let them pick your dish!

PLACE PICTURE HERE

PLACE PICTURE HERE

$Costs range from $25-$50

Culture & More Adventure

$ Challenge #1

> Not your ordinary hike! Visit Turkey Run State Park and take in nature's beauty. Don't forget your camera!

$$ Challenge #2

> Visit Conner Prairie and soar high on the 1859 Balloon Voyage!

$$$ Challenge #3

> Tour Marengo Cave or spend the night!

IOWA

TOP CITIES: Des Moines, Iowa City, Cedar Rapids, Davenport, Sioux City
BEST TIME TO TRAVEL: Summer, Fall (August)
SIGNATURE DRINKS: Busch Beer, Frozen Blue Water Margarita, Templeton Rye on the rocks
HIDDEN GEMS: American Gothic Barn Mount Vernon
BUCKET LIST: Grotto of the Redemption, Capitol Building, Prairie Lights
FESTIVALS: Iowa State Fair, RAGBRAI, The Quad City Times Bix 7, Tulip Time Festival, Burlington Steamboat Days, Des Moines Arts Festival

$Costs range from $5-$250

Activities

$ Challenge #1

> Take an evening bike ride on the High Trestle Trail. Make a stop between Ankeny and Woodward and take in the views of the High Trestle Bridge.

$$ Challenge #2

> Walk the Lover's Leap Swinging Bridge.

$$$ Challenge #3

> Take a private champagne hot air balloon ride over the city.

PLACE PICTURE HERE

IOWA

$Costs range from $5-$300

Food & Drinks

$ Challenge #1

> Eat like a local! Local food favorites: persimmon pudding, pork tenderloin sandwich, sugar cream pie, Coney dog, triple XXX root beer, Just Pop In popcorn, fried biscuits with apple butter.

$$ Challenge #2

> Taste the freshness! Do an authentic farm-to-table experience at one of the eight locations.

$$$ Challenge #3

> Have a tea party on a farm. Visit Miss Spenser's Tea Room in New Virginia.

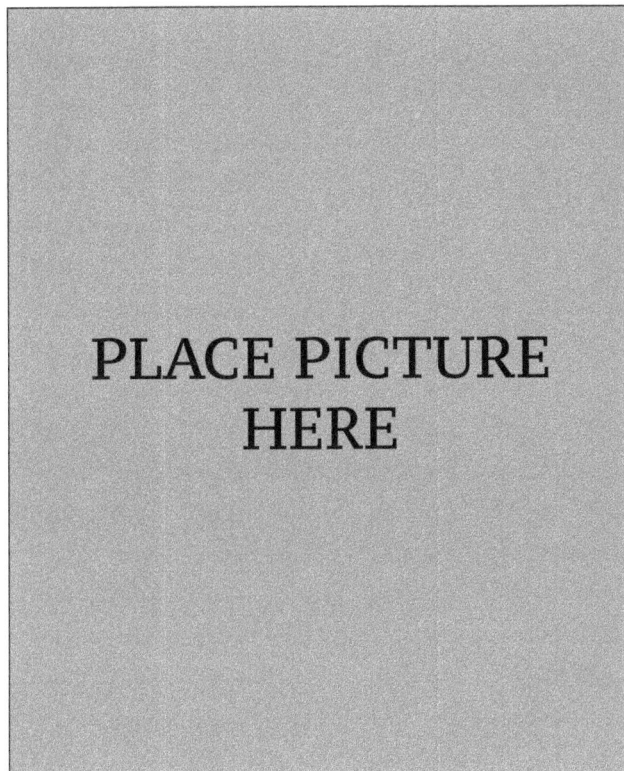

PLACE PICTURE HERE

PLACE PICTURE HERE

$Costs range from $15-$89

Culture & More Adventure

$ Challenge #1

> Flower power! Grab the camera and visit the Greater Des Moines Botanical Garden.

$$ Challenge #2

> Hop on a canoe and paddle down the upper Iowa River in northeast Iowa.

$$$ Challenge #3

> Rock climb the majestic midwest at Iowa's Pictured Rocks.

KANSAS

TOP CITIES: Wichita, Topeka, Overland Park, Lawrence, Manhattan, Pittsburg
BEST TIME TO TRAVEL: Summer, Fall (June–September)
SIGNATURE DRINKS: Fireball, Vignoles wine spritzer, Horsefeather (J. Rieger & Co. KC Whiskey, ginger beer, Angostura bitters)
HIDDEN GEMS: OZ Museum, Truckhenge Farm in Topeka, Explore the Strataca Salt Museum, Visit the Garden of Eden in Lucas
BUCKET LIST: Deanna Rose Children's Farmstead
FESTIVALS: Dancefestopia Music Festival, Kansas State Fair, Longton Fall Festival, Great American Market, High Plains Music Fest

$Costs range from $10-$85

Activities

$ Challenge #1

➢ Watch the sunset at Clinton Lake.

$$ Challenge #2

➢ Looking for scenic views? Take a day trip to the Arikaree Breaks badlands to see nature at its best.

$$$ Challenge #3

➢ Go canoeing on the Kansas River Trail.

PLACE PICTURE HERE

KANSAS

$Costs range from $15-$75

Food & Drinks

$ Challenge #1

➤ Eat like a local! Local food favorites: Kansas City Pig & Swig Sandwich, BBQ, BBQ hot wings, country fried steak, Z-Man sandwich, brown bread frozen ice cream, bierocks, grebble, sour cream and raisin pie.

$$ Challenge #2

➤ Do a late night taco run on the Boulevard.

$$$ Challenge #3

➤ Go bar hopping and let locals place your drink order based on their Kansas favorites!

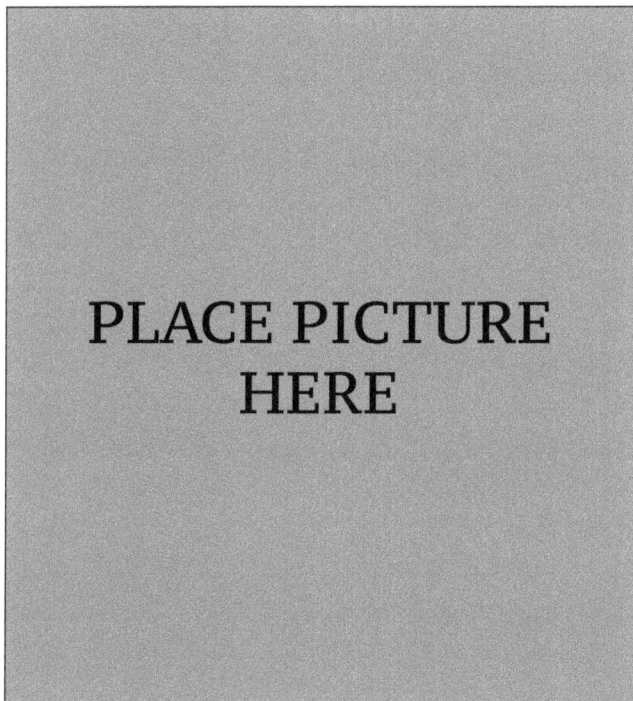

PLACE PICTURE HERE

PLACE PICTURE HERE

$Costs range from $10-$40

Culture & More Adventure

$ Challenge #1

➤ Take in some art at the NOTO Arts & Entertainment District.

$$ Challenge #2

➤ Instaworthy! Visit Kansas City Library's Giant Bookshelf and take some fun pictures.

$$$ Challenge #3

➤ Instaworthy! Visit one or all of the following to take some iconic pictures: Mushroom Rock, 1950s All-Electric House, Monument Rocks.

KENTUCKY

TOP CITIES: Louisville, Lexington, Bowling Green, Frankfort
BEST TIME TO TRAVEL: Spring (April-May), Fall (September-October)
SIGNATURE DRINKS: Kentucky straight bourbon whiskey, Mint Julep (mint leaves, simple syrup, bourbon, Angostura bitters)
HIDDEN GEMS: Dinosaur World, The Abbey of Gethsemani, Kentucky Castle in Versailles
BUCKET LIST: Cumberland Falls, Wigwam Village #2 in Cave City
FESTIVALS: Kentucky Derby, Kentucky State Fair, Kentucky State BBQ Festival, Kentucky Bourbon Festival, Bourbon & Beyond, Terrapin Hill Harvest Festival

$Costs range from $50-$150

Activities

$ Challenge #1

➢ Go horseback riding in Mammoth Cave National Park.

$$ Challenge #2

➢ Visit the Maker's Mark Distillery and dip the bottle in the signature red wax. Make sure you try the bourbon flavored whole-bean coffee chocolates and cherries.

$$$ Challenge #3

➢ Try underground paddling with the Cavern Glow Adventure experience.

PLACE PICTURE HERE

KENTUCKY

$Costs range from $55-$85

Food & Drinks

$ Challenge #1

➤ Take a sip at all of the distilleries on the Bourbon trail. Don't forget to collect some gourmet souvenirs to take back home!

$$ Challenge #2

➤ Go bar hopping to find out who makes the best Mint Julep drink.

$$$ Challenge #3

➤ Eat like a local! Try the following local food favorites: derby pie, Kentucky Hot Brown, thoroughbred pie, caramel biscuits, and don't forget to try some moonshine, transparent puddings & pies, bourbon balls,Shaker lemon pie, burgoo.

PLACE PICTURE HERE

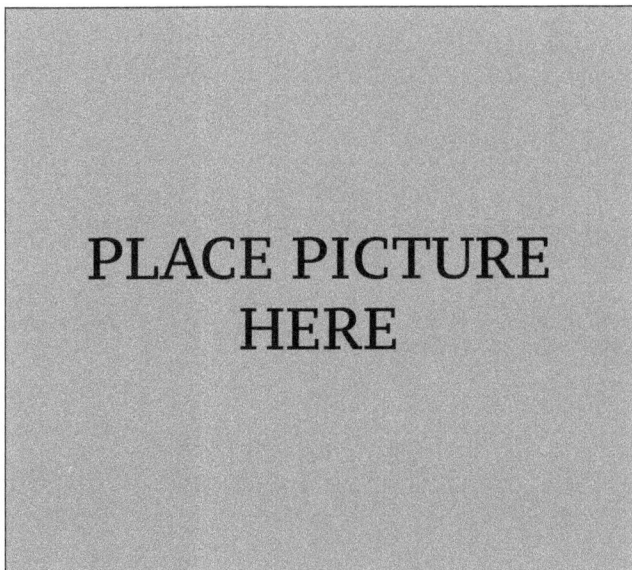

PLACE PICTURE HERE

$Costs range from $5-$300

Culture & More Adventure

$ Challenge #1

➤ Visit the Kentucky Artisan Center for exhibitions and art performances.

$$ Challenge #2

➤ Take a hike on Black Mountain.

$$$ Challenge #3

➤ Bet on the horses! Visit the Churchill Downs, home of the Kentucky Derby, and place a few bets on the horses.

LOUISIANA

TOP CITIES: New Orleans, Baton Rouge, Lafayette
BEST TIME TO TRAVEL: Spring (February-May), Winter (December-January)
SIGNATURE DRINKS: Sazerac, Hurricane (light rum, dark rum, fresh lime juice, fresh orange juice, passionfruit puree, simple syrup, grenadine)
HIDDEN GEMS: Palace Market Frenchmen art gallery, Victorian Mansion, Audubon Park
BUCKET LIST: French Quarter, Bourbon St, Swamp airboat ride, See the iconic St. Roch Chapel, Hang out in the Garden District, Go off the beaten path and take a ferry from New Orleans to Algiers
FESTIVALS: Mardi Gras, Essence Festival, Jazz Festival, French Quarter Festival, Breaux Bridge Crawfish Festival, Tennessee Williams New Orleans Literary Festival

$Costs range from $5-$125

<u>Activities</u>

$ Challenge #1

➢ Support the local artists! Visit the open-air night artist market on Frenchmen St, New Orleans.

$$ Challenge #2

➢ Hop on a light-up bike and take a self-guided tour around New Orleans. Don't be afraid to get lost!

$$$ Challenge #3

➢ Take an airboat swamp tour to see some alligators.

PLACE PICTURE HERE

LOUISIANA

Food & Drinks

$ Challenge #1

- ➢ Eat like a local! Local food favorites: jambalaya, beignets, shrimp po' boy, crawfish boil, blackened fish, doberge cake, cracklins, gumbo, king cake, etouffee, snowballs, turtle soup, alligator, boudin, bananas foster French toast.

$$ Challenge #2

- ➢ Take a day trip to the Bayous and go shrimping.

$$$ Challenge #3

- ➢ Take a cajun cooking class and learn how to make some local dishes.

PLACE PICTURE HERE

PLACE PICTURE HERE

Culture & More Adventure

$ Challenge #1

- ➢ Hop on a streetcar and check out the local boutiques, costume shops, and art galleries on Magazine Street.

$$ Challenge #2

- ➢ Take a break from the partying and visit one of the local museums: New Orleans Museum of Art, National WWII Museum, Backstreet Cultural Museum, New Orleans Pharmacy Museum.

$$$ Challenge #3

- ➢ Step outside of the norm and visit one of the 42 Historic Cemeteries of New Orleans.

MAINE

TOP CITIES: Portland, Bangor, Bar Harbor
BEST TIME TO TRAVEL: Fall (September-October), Winter (November–May)
SIGNATURE DRINK: Allen's Coffee Brandy & Milk
HIDDEN GEMS: New England road trip, Moose Point State Park, Puffin Watching
BUCKET LIST: Laite Memorial Beach, Old Orchard Beach, Kayak to the 50+ islands of Merchant's Row, Hike inside the Greenwood or Debsconeag ice caves, Dig for clams, Learn to sail, Sea kayaking and island hopping in Acadia National Park
FESTIVALS: Maine Boating Festival, The Kennebunkport Festival, North Atlantic Blues Festivals, Maine Lobster Festival

$Costs range from $75-$230

Activities

$ Challenge #1

- ➤ Make it your mission to find a lighthouse and take a selfie! Tip: the Portland Head Lighthouse is very popular.

$$ Challenge #2

- ➤ Hike Tumbledown Mountain, and once you reach the top make sure you stop for a quick refreshing swim!

$$$ Challenge #3

- ➤ Ice ice baby! Go ice fishing in the winter.

PLACE PICTURE HERE

MAINE

$Costs range from $50-$99

Food & Drinks

$ Challenge #1

➢ Go lobster boating and take a cooking class on how to cook a Maine Lobster.

$$ Challenge #2

➢ Seek out and attend a clam bake.

$$$ Challenge #3

➢ Eat like a local! Local food favorites: lobster corned hake, fiddleheads, ramps, moose, Kennebec potato, seadog biscuits, Indian pudding, whoopie pies, lobster pie, clam roll, Moxie.

PLACE PICTURE HERE

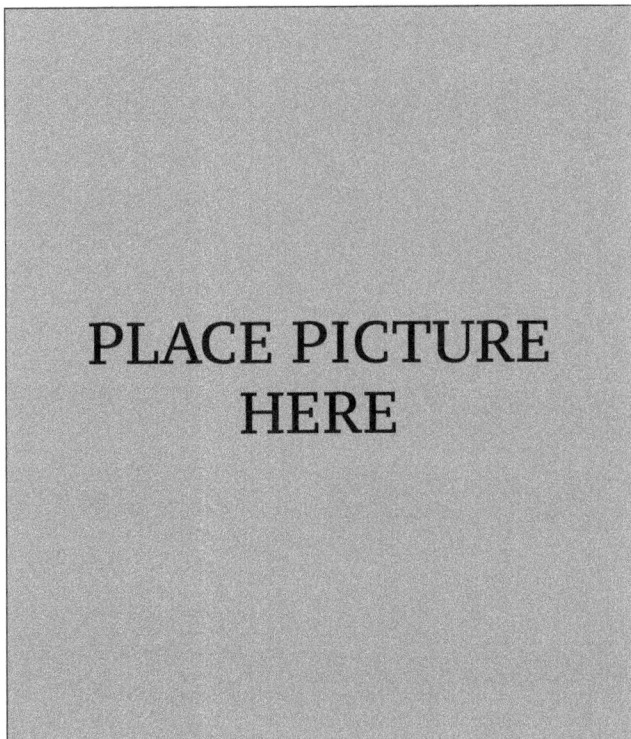

PLACE PICTURE HERE

$Costs range from $15-$300

Culture & More Adventure

$ Challenge #1

➢ Hike Cadillac Mountain and watch the first sunrise in the United States.

$$ Challenge #2

➢ Go snowmobiling from Kittery to Fort Kent on the Maine ITS snowmobile trail system.

$$$ Challenge #3

➢ Take a guided moose safari canoe trip or go whale watching on the coast.

MARYLAND

TOP CITIES: Baltimore, Annapolis, Washington D.C., Columbia, Germantown
BEST TIME TO TRAVEL: Spring (March-May), Fall (September-November))
SIGNATURE DRINKS: Orange Crush, Back-Eyed Susan (orange juice, pineapple juice, vodka, rum), The Rickey (gin, lime, soda water)
HIDDEN GEMS: Greenwell State Park, Great Falls Park
BUCKET LIST: Paddle Blackwater, the Everglades, Take a water taxi on the Baltimore Harbor, National Museum of African American History & Culture, American Visionary Art Museum, Visit downtown Annapolis and Ego Alley
FESTIVALS: Baltimore Seafood Festival, Brunch Fest, Baltimore Rhythm Festival, Maryland Wine Festival, Mermaid's Kiss Oyster Fest, Maryland Crab Fest, Giant National Capital Barbecue Battle

$Costs range from $5-$250

Activities

$ Challenge #1

➤ Go to Assateague State Park to sit on the beach and watch the sunrise and the wild horses run.

$$ Challenge #2

➤ Stand up paddle board or kayak the Chesapeake Bay.

$$$ Challenge #3

➤ Go scuba diving at the national aquarium.

PLACE PICTURE HERE

MARYLAND

$Costs range from $25-$80

Food & Drinks

$ Challenge #1

➢ Eat like a local! Try some local food favorites: Crabby Bloody Mary, steamed crabs, crab cakes, Utz crab-flavored potato chips, Thrasher's French fries, Natty Boh lager, pit beef, Berger Cookies, Smith Island cake, Fisher's popcorn, soft shell crab, cream of crab soup, snowballs, oysters, Coddies, crab dip.

$$ Challenge #2

➢ Visit all eight of the Maryland wine trails.

$$$ Challenge #3

➢ Create a unique dining experience! Find a beachfront resturant and eat some fresh seafood.

PLACE PICTURE HERE

PLACE PICTURE HERE

$Costs range from $15-$90

Culture & More Adventure

$ Challenge #1

➢ Enjoy a nice day or night walk on the Ocean City Boardwalk to shop, eat, and drink.

$$ Challenge #2

➢ Hop on a bike and ride through the C&O Canal Towpath.

$$$ Challenge #3

➢ Go fossil hunting on Calvert Cliffs State Park. Bonus points if you find shark teeth!

MASSACHUSETTS

TOP CITIES: Boston, Cape Cod, Martha's Vineyard, Nantucket, Plymouth, Cambridge, Provincetown, Salem
BEST TIME TO TRAVEL: Summer, Fall (June–October)
SIGNATURE DRINKS: Sam Adams, Cape Codder (vodka, cranberry juice, lime wedge)
HIDDEN GEMS: Freedom Trail, Yankee Candle Village, Museum of Bad Art, Joseph Sylvia State Park
BUCKET LIST: Visit Plymouth Rock, Salem Witch Museum during Halloween week, Kayak the Charles River on the fourth of July
FESTIVALS: Honey Harvest, Frog Pond Pumpkin Float, Mayfair, BAMS Fest, The Big E, Martha's Vineyard Food & Wine Festival, Head of the Charles Regatta

$Costs range from $15-$300

Activities

$ Challenge #1

➤ Take a trip to Coast Guard Beach in Cape Cod.

$$ Challenge #2

➤ Go fishing or hiking at the Quabbin Reservoir.

$$$ Challenge #3

➤ Do a day trip to Martha's Vineyard Island.

PLACE PICTURE HERE

MASSACHUSETTS

Food & Drinks

$ Challenge #1

> Eat like a local! Try some local food favorites: clam chowder, lobster roll, cannolis, baked beans, Boston cream pie, Fenway Frank, fried clams, grapenut custard, grilled blueberry muffins, apple cider donuts, baked stuffed scrod, scallops, coffee gelatin.

$$ Challenge #2

> Ask a local! Get a recommendation for a locally owned restaurant and try as many dishes as your stomach will allow.

$$$ Challenge #3

> Find a local sugar shack and take home some fresh maple syrup as a souvenir.

PLACE PICTURE HERE

PLACE PICTURE HERE

$Costs range from $10-$60

Culture & More Adventure

$ Challenge #1

> Go bike riding and explore while taking in the views at the Shining Sea Bikeway.

$$ Challenge #2

> Act like a tourist! Visit the Mapparium and the Brattle Book Shop and check them off on your bucket list.

$$$ Challenge #3

> Life is but a fairy tail! Dare to experience something out of the ordinary and take a trip to Santarella Gingerbread House.

MICHIGAN

TOP CITIES: Detroit, Grand Rapids, Traverse City, Mackinac Island, Holland, Saugatuck, Ann Arbor

BEST TIME TO TRAVEL: Spring, Summer, Fall (May-October)

SIGNATURE DRINKS: Oberon, Last Word (gin, fresh squeezed lime juice, Green Chartreuse, Luxardo Maraschino), The Hummer (white rum, Kahlua, vanilla ice cream)

HIDDEN GEMS: Ocqueoc Falls State Forest Campground, Bronner's Christmas Wonderland, Tahquamenon Falls, Murals in the Market, Silver Lake Dunes, Arcadia Dunes, Manitou Island

BUCKET LIST: Mackinac Bridge, Sunset Park Ice Pole, Leland's Historic Fishtown, Arch Rock on Mackinac Island, Diving or canoeing at Rising Sun Shipwreck, Little Venice, Kitch-iti-kipi, Les Cheneaux Islands, Marvin's Marvelous Mechanical Museum

FESTIVALS: Tulip Time Festival, ArtPrize International Art Show, Electric Forest Festival, Movement Electronic Music Festival, Common Ground Festival, Detroit International Jazz Festival, Mo Pop Festival, Faster Horses Festival

---

$Costs range from $10-$85

Activities

$ Challenge #1

> Visit Sleeping Bear Dunes. You can swim at the beach, attempt to run up the sand dunes, or bodysurf.

$$ Challenge #2

> Instaworthy! Grab the camera and visit Pictured Rocks National Lakeshore. Explore beautiful rock formations, hike the forest, and enjoy the waterfalls.

$$$ Challenge #3

> Go beach hopping and experience some of the Great Lakes such as Empire or South Haven. Extra bonus points if you make time to watch the sunrise over Lake Huron or watch the sunset over Lake Michigan.

PLACE PICTURE HERE

MICHIGAN

Food & Drinks

$ Challenge #1

➤ Eat like a local! Try some local food favorites: Detroit-style pizza, hot fudge cream puff, corned beef Dinty Moore sandwich, paczki, Detroit Street Brick, Cudighi, Mackinac Island fudge, Coney dog, pierogi, venison.

$$ Challenge #2

➤ Drink like a local! Try these popular Detroit drinks: Hummer Cocktail, Faygo Pop, Ghettoblaster, Stroh's beer, Vernors soda, Boston Cooler, cider, and don't forget the donuts with your drink!

$$$ Challenge #3

➤ Treat yourself to a fine dining experience and find a resturant with a skyline view. Visit www.TheTravelBella.com for recommendations.

PLACE PICTURE HERE

PLACE PICTURE HERE

$Costs range from $5-$125

Culture & More Adventure

$ Challenge #1

➤ Take a leap of faith! Go cliff jumping off Blackrocks in Marquette's Presque Isle Park lakeshore.

$$ Challenge #2

➤ Not just another kayak experience! For a one-of-a-kind experience, kayak to Turnip Rock.

$$$ Challenge #3

➤ Visit Saugatuck, Michigan's artist colony and beach destination known for dune schooners. Hop on a buggy and ride it through the high dunes!

MINNESOTA

TOP CITIES: Minneapolis, Saint Paul, Rochester, Bloomington, Brooklyn Park, Duluth, Plymouth
BEST TIME TO TRAVEL: Spring, Summer, Fall (May-September)
SIGNATURE DRINKS: Beertini/Midwest Martini, Bootleg (vodka or gin, frozen limeade, frozen lemonade, fresh mint, simple syrup, club soda)
HIDDEN GEMS: Devil's Kettle, Niagara Cave, Hidden Beach
BUCKET LIST: Mall of America, Split Rock Lighthouse, The Cocktail Room
FESTIVALS: Uptown Food Truck Festival, Minnesota Monthly GrillFest, Whiskey Tasting Festival, European Christmas Market

$Costs range from $55-$275

Activity

$ Challenge #1

> Go water skiing at one of Minnesota's many lakes.

$$ Challenge #2

> Go exploring at Boundary Waters Canoe Area Wilderness. The picturesque sights will have you believing that you are no longer in the United States. Need a tour guide? Hop on a dogsled and let them lead the way.

$$$ Challenge #3

> Visit Lake Harriet and learn how to sail.

PLACE PICTURE HERE

MINNESOTA

Food & Drinks

$ Challenge #1

➢ Visit various restaurants to try their version of the famous "Juicy Lucy" and afterward, visit The Cocktail Room to enjoy a craft drink.

$$ Challenge #2

➢ Handpick your own fresh fruit at a local u-pick farm.

$$$ Challenge #3

➢ Need a handful of options for lunch or dinner? Visit Midtown Global Market or Keg and Case Market and try as many local vendors as you can.

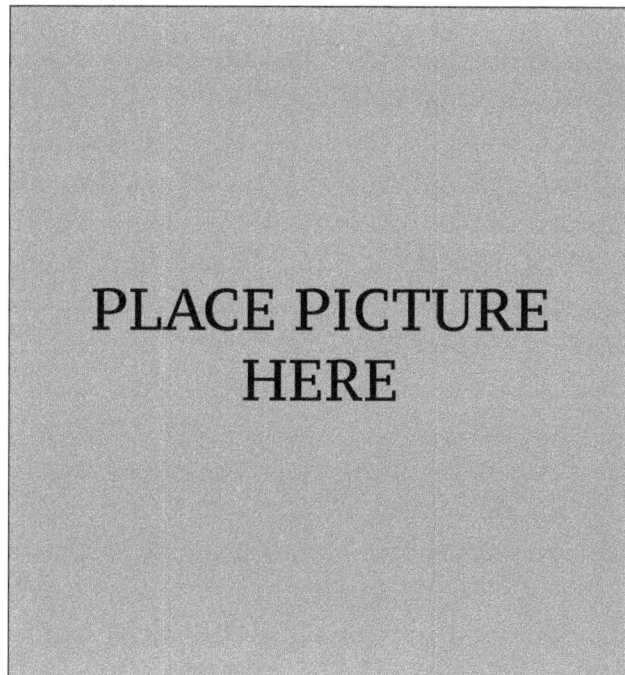

PLACE PICTURE HERE

PLACE PICTURE HERE

Culture & More Adventure

$ Challenge #1

➢ Take a walk in the depths of one of the midwest's largest caves, Niagara Cave.

$$ Challenge #2

➢ Rent a car and take the drive of a lifetime, coasting the North Shore and taking in nature's beauty.

$$$ Challenge #3

➢ Spend a night in one of Minnesota's unique lodging options ranging from treehouses, lighthouses, houseboats or tugboats.

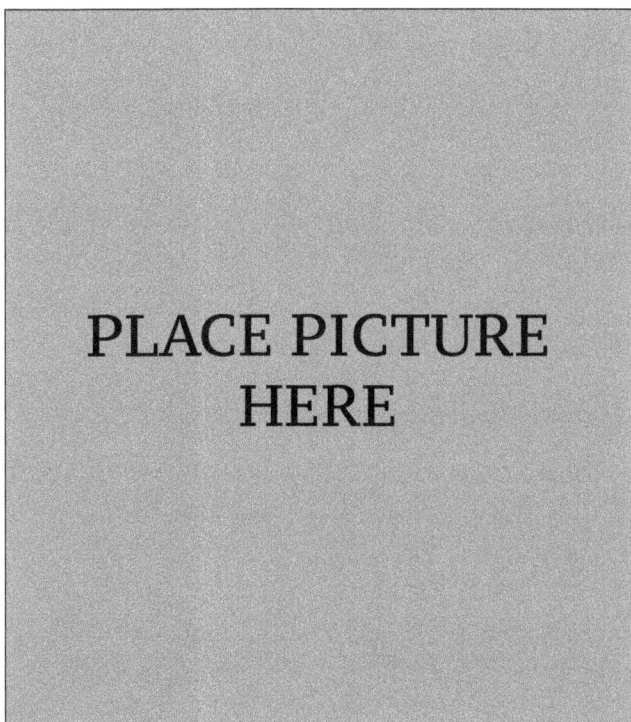

MISSISSIPPI

TOP CITIES: Biloxi, Jackson, Natchez, Gulf Port, South Haven, Hattisburg, Maddison
BEST TIME TO TRAVEL: Spring (March–May), Fall (September–November)
SIGNATUR DRINKS: Mississippi Punch (dry muscadine wine, bourbon, orange juice, cranberry juice, fresh lime, grenadine, club soda), Mississippi Mud Martini (RumChata, vodka, Kahlua, chocolate syrup, chocolate cookie wafers)
HIDDEN GEMS: Mississippi's "Little Grand Canyon", Cooper Falls, Natchez Trace
BUCKET LIST: Mississippi River paddle streamer cruise
FESTIVALS: Juke Joint Festival, Down Home Music Festival, Mighty Roots Music Festival

$Costs range from $35-$300

Activities

$ Challenge #1

➤ Visit Biloxi Beach, "The Playground of the South", and take a shrimping trip along the Gulf Cost.

$$ Challenge #2

➤ Take a ferry or do an excursion cruise and spend the day on Ship Island.

$$$ Challenge #3

➤ Charter a Catalina sailboat and spend a relaxing day sailing.

PLACE PICTURE HERE

MISSISSIPPI

$Costs range from $5-$120

Food & Drinks

$ Challenge #1

> Eat like a local! Try some local food favorites: hot tamales, fried green tomatoes, chicken and dumplings, Mississippi mud pie, pecan pie, Cajun fried pecans, crawfish, boiled peanuts, deer meat, catfish, Gulf shrimp, kibbe, pompano, blue crab, po' boys, comeback sauce, caramel cake.

$$ Challenge #2

> Get a recommendation from a local for breakfast, lunch, and dinner for the day.

$$$ Challenge #3

> Visit the Mississippi Agriculture & Forestry Museum to understand how food is made in America, and pick up an old-time treat at the General Store.

PLACE PICTURE HERE

PLACE PICTURE HERE

$Costs range from $15-$80

Culture & More Adventure

$ Challenge #1

> Grab the camera, put on your best high-fashion outfit and visit the historic Windsor Ruins for a mini photoshoot.

$$ Challenge #2

> Visit Tupelo, Elvis Presley's birthplace, and take a tour of his childhood home.

$$$ Challenge #3

> Visit the Biloxi Lighthouse to take in views of the Gulf of Mexico.

MISSOURI

TOP CITIES: St. Louis, Branson, Kansas City, Table Rock Lake, Lake of the Ozarks, Hannibal
BEST TIME TO TRAVEL: Fall, Winter (September–December)
SIGNATURE DRINKS: Budweiser/Bud Light, The Horsefeather (whiskey, ginger beer, lemon), Caribou Lou (151 proof rum, coconut rum, pineapple juice)
HIDDEN GEMS: Stark Caverns, Alley Spring Grist Mill Historical Site, Tiger Sanctuary, Arabia Steamboat Museum, Bloch Building, Onondaga Cave
BUCKET LIST: The City of Hannibal, Gateway Arch, Nelson Atkins Museum
FESTIVALS: Trails West Festival, LouFest Music Festival, Red, White & Blue BBQ Blowout

$Costs range from $25-$275

Activities

$ Challenge #1

➢ Hop on a tram and take it to the top of Gateway Arch.

$$ Challenge #2 (Christmas Season)

➢ Visit the Missouri Botanical Garden in St. Louis during the holiday season at night to take in the beauty of the garden and the glowing lights.

$$$ Challenge #3

➢ Feeling adventurous? Go cave diving at Bonne Terre Mine.

PLACE PICTURE HERE

MISSOURI

Food & Drinks

$ Challenge #1

> Ask a local to recommend the best BBQ restaurant to try.

$$ Challenge #2

> Eat like a local! Try some local food favorites: burnt ends, gooey butter cake, St. Louis-style pizza, Provel, cheese curds, ribs, Red Hot Riplets, St. Paul sandwich, Abraxas beer, pork steak, frozen custard, Fitz's Root Beer float, toasted ravioli, bionic apples.

$$$ Challenge #3

> Visit a farm and indulge in the experience of a Missouri Barn Dinner.

PLACE PICTURE HERE

PLACE PICTURE HERE

$Costs range from $35-$120

Culture & More Adventure

$ Challenge #1

> Take a hike or a swim in Meramec State Park.

$$ Challenge #2

> Visit Bat Bar in the Lost Canyon Cave in Ridgedale. Hop on a golf cart and ride it to the top to take in amazing views and good drinks.

$$$ Challenge #3

> Take a unique tour and enjoy wine tasting in a cave at the Cave Vineyard & Distillery.

MONTANA

TOP CITIES: Bozeman, Helena, Glacier National Park, Livingston, Missoula, Whitefish, Great Falls

BEST TIME TO TRAVEL: Summer (July, August), Winter (December, March)

SIGNATURE DRINKS: Moscow Mules, Boilermaker (shot of whiskey in a pint of beer), Whiskey Ditch (whiskey, water)

HIDDEN GEMS: Boiling River, Sand Creek Clydesdales Ranch, Bleu Horses at Three Forks, Makoshika State Park, Missouri Headwaters State Park, Maddison Buffalo Jump State Park, Yaak Valley

BUCKET LIST: Yellowstone National Park, Berkley Pit, Flathead Lake, Grasshopper Glacier, Tubing through Downtown Missoula, Riding Rocks

FESTIVALS: Gallatin River Fly Fishing Festival, Montana Dragon Boat Festival, Bikes Brews & Blues Festival, Winter Festival, Whitefish Winter Carnival, Under the Big Sky Festival, Red Ants Pants Music Festival

$Costs range from $5-$60

Activities

$ Challenge #1

- ➢ Head to the Garden of One Thousand Buddhas for a one-of-a-kind spiritual experience.

$$ Challenge #2

- ➢ Grab the camera and spend the day at Beartooth Mountain.

$$$ Challenge #3

- ➢ Take a hike to Iceberg Lake in Glacier National Park.

PLACE PICTURE HERE

MONTANA

$Costs range from $15-$45

Food & Drinks

$ Challenge #1

> Eat like a local! Try some local food favorites: huckleberry shake, Pickle Barrel sandwiches, elk burgers, bison burgers, huckleberry swirls, fry bread, chokecherries, grizzly paws, Catholic burgers.

$$ Challenge #2

> Go bar hopping and try the local drink known as the Boilermaker, aka the "Sean O'Farrell and the whiskey ditch".

$$$ Challenge #3

> Ask a local to recommend a locally owned resturant.

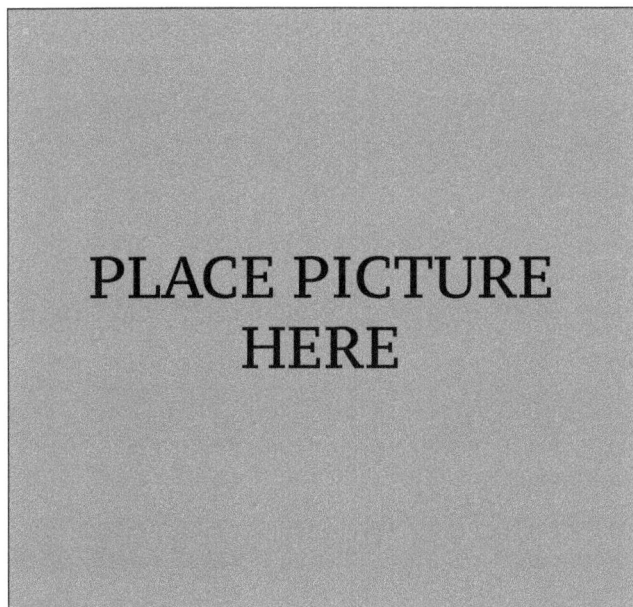

PLACE PICTURE HERE

PLACE PICTURE HERE

$Costs range from $25-$99

Culture & More Adventure

$ Challenge #1

> Go paddle boarding on Lake McDonald. Don't forget to snap a picture on the paddle board with the mountains behind you.

$$ Challenge #2

> Take a scenic mountain drive on the Going-to-the-Sun Road.

$$$ Challenge #3

> Take a wintertime dive to the National Bison Range to take some scenic pictures.

NEBRASKA

TOP CITIES: Omaha, Kearney, Lincoln, Grand Island, Lake McConaughy, Bellevue
BEST TIME TO TRAVEL: Summer, Fall (May–October)
SIGNATURE DRINKS: Black Betty Imperial Stout, Red Beer
HIDDEN GEMS: The Hastings Museum Kool-Aid Exhibit, Toadstool Geologic Park
BUCKET LIST: Chimney Rock, Attend the Annual Nebraska Star Party, Ponca State Park, Sunken Gardens, Visit Platte River Valley and watch the sandhill crane migration during the springtime
FESTIVALS: R&B Love Festival, Crane Watch Festival, Holiday Lights Festival, Nebraska Balloon & Wine Festival

$Costs range from $20-$140

Activities

$ Challenge #1

> It's time for a photoshoot! Put on your Sunday best and take a visit to Carhenge in Alliance.

$$ Challenge #2

> Go tanking on Loup River.

$$$ Challenge #3

> Cliff dive into Gallagher Lake.

PLACE PICTURE HERE

NEBRASKA

$Costs range from $15-$85

Food & Drinks

$ Challenge #1

➤ Eat like a local! Try some local food favorites: pork tenderloin sandwich, Rocky Mountain oysters, raisin pie, ribs, bone-in ribeye steak, Cheese Fenchees, Reuben sandwiches, Butter Brickle ice cream, chicken fried steak, Omaha-style pizza, Stromer sandwich.

$$ Challenge #2

➤ Take a food & history tour to indulge in the culture of Nebraska.

$$$ Challenge #3

➤ Spend the day in the Old Market and sample food and drinks from the local busineses.

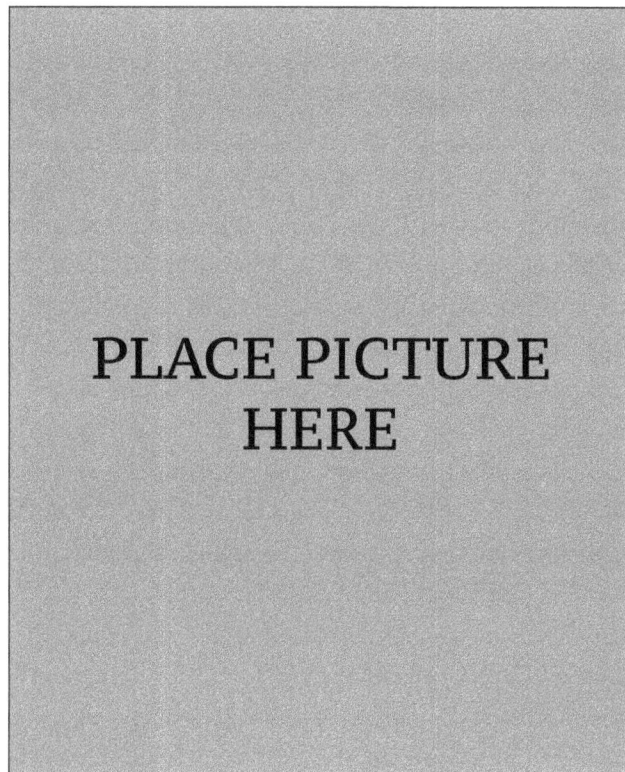

PLACE PICTURE HERE

PLACE PICTURE HERE

$Costs range from $25-$150

Culture & More Adventure

$ Challenge #1

➤ Take a bike ride on the Cowboy Trail.

$$ Challenge #2

➤ Go canoeing on the Niobrara river.

$$$ Challenge #3

➤ Hop on a gondola in Heartland of America Park, Omaha, and take in the scenery.

NEVADA

TOP CITIES: Las Vegas, Reno, Carson City, Boulder City
BEST TIME TO TRAVEL: Fall, Spring (October–April)
SIGNATURE DRINKS: Picon Punch (Amer Picon Liqueur, soda water, grenadine, splash of lemon and brandy), Nevada Cocktail (light rum, grapefruit juice, lime juice, a dash of bitters)
HIDDEN GEMS: Valley of Fire State Park, Lunar Crater National Natural Landmark, Great Basin National Park, Fly Geyser, Erotic Heritage Museum, Pyramid Lake, The Mojave Desert
BUCKET LIST: Lake Tahoe, Hoover Dam air tour, Lake Mead, Grand Canyon, Experience a Las Vegas show on The Strip, Book a penthouse for one night in Vegas
FESTIVALS: RiSE Lantern Festival, Burning Man, Helldorado days, Psycho Fest, Reggae Rise Up, Life is Beautiful Festival, Lantern Fest

---

$Costs range from $20-$65

Activities

$ Challenge #1

➢ Get away from the craziness of the strip and take a drive to the ghost town of Rhyolite to experience the Goldwell Open Air Museum for art.

$$ Challenge #2

➢ Fly like superman and go ziplining over Fremont Street. Afterward, explore everything that Fremont Street has to offer.

$$$ Challenge #3

➢ Grab the camera and do a fun photoshoot at the Neon Boneyard.

PLACE PICTURE HERE

NEVADA

$Costs range from $5-$300

Food & Drinks

$ Challenge #1

- ➢ Look up or ask around what the top buffet is on The Strip and spend the afternoon indulging in good food. Not into the buffet? Go on a scavenger hunt for the best taco food truck or eat at a celebrity chef restaurant.

$$ Challenge #2

- ➢ Take a mixology class to create or learn some signature drinks.

$$$ Challenge #3

- ➢ Ice ice baby! Ever drink out of a glass made completely out of ice? Well, head to the minus5 Ice Bar, put on a fur, and drink for as long as you can withstand the cold.

PLACE PICTURE HERE

PLACE PICTURE HERE

$Costs range from $30-$125

Culture & More Adventure

$ Challenge #1

- ➢ Try something out of the ordinary and visit "Dig This" Heavy Equipment Playground for the ultimate bulldozer or excavator experience!

$$ Challenge #2

- ➢ Take a cooking class and cook like a celebrity chef.

$$$ Challenge #3

- ➢ Go skyjumping from the SkyPod at the STRAT!

NEW HAMPSHIRE

TOP CITIES: Manchester, Portsmouth, Exeter, Hanover, Harrisville, Jackson, Keene, Littleton, Meredith, Petertborough, Portsmouth, Sugar Hill
BEST TIME TO TRAVEL: Summer (June-August)
SIGNATURE DRINKS: Bud Light, Hard Cider
HIDDEN GEMS: Flume Gorge in Franconia Notch State Park, Mount Washington Cog Railway (The Cog), Frost Point, Cat Alley
BUCKET LIST: Watch fireworks at Hampton Beach, Visit the Isle of Shoals, The Basin Waterfall, Americas Stonehenge, Ice Castles (winter season)
FESTIVALS: New Hampshire Magazines Best of NH Party, American Independence Festival, White Mountain Boogie N' Blues Festival, Hampton Beach Seafood Festival

$Costs range from $20-$125

Activities

$ Challenge #1

➤ Visit an orchard and go apple picking, then go on a treasure hunt for the best apple cider donut.

$$ Challenge #2

➤ Need a dose of nature? Take a hike at Mount Monadnock.

$$$ Challenge #3

➤ Road trip! Rent a car and take an epic road trip on the Mount Washington Auto Road.

PLACE PICTURE HERE

NEW HAMPSHIRE

Food & Drinks

$ Challenge #1

➤ Eat like a local! Try some local food favorites: lobster roll, New England clam chowder, maple walnut ice cream, fried lake bass, apple cider cocktails, apple wine, pancakes with maple syrup, steamers, maple sundae, sugar in the snow.

$$ Challenge #2

➤ Take advantage of a wine maker's tour.

$$$ Challenge #3

➤ Ask a local to recommend the best locally owned resturant and let them pick your dish.

PLACE PICTURE HERE

PLACE PICTURE HERE

Culture & More Adventure

$ Challenge #1

➤ Take a stroll on the Moat Mountain trail and have a soak in Diana's Baths.

$$ Challenge #2

➤ Grab the camera and tiptoe through the tulips at the Wicked Tulips flower farm.

$$$ Challenge #3

➤ Feeling extremely adventurous? Go swimming in an isolated swimming hole... clothing optional.

NEW JERSEY

TOP CITIES: Atlantic Station, Jersey City, Trenton, Newark, Princeton, Cape May, Hoboken, Ocean City, Wildwood, Asbury Park, Morristown
BEST TIME TO TRAVEL: Spring, Summer (April–June)
SIGNATURE DRINKS: Jaeger Bombs, Pina Colada, Jack Rose (apple brandy, lemon juice, grenadine)
HIDDEN GEMS: Buttermilk Falls State Park, Sunset Beach in Cape May
BUCKET LIST: Visit the Jersey Shore, Experience the Grounds For Sculpture museum, sculpture garden & arboretum, Ride the Jersey Devil - the world's tallest, longest and fastest roller coaster at Six Flags, Atlantic City Boardwalk
FESTIVALS: Atlantic City Beer and Music Festival, Bamboozle Festival, River Fest Food and Music Festival, Lighthouse International Film Festival, Barefoot Country Music Fest

$Costs range from $25-$65

Activity

$ Challenge #1

➢ Go kayaking on the Hudson.

$$ Challenge #2

➢ Find a lighthouse and climb to the top for a great photo op.

$$$ Challenge #3

➢ Visit Asbury Park and hop on a swan pedal boat and pedal away.

PLACE PICTURE HERE

NEW JERSEY

Food & Drinks

$ Challenge #1

➢ Eat like a local! Try some local food favorites: Taylor ham/pork roll, Italian hot dog, tomato pie, Sloppy Joe, saltwater taffy, hoagies.

$$ Challenge #2

➢ For some of the best seafood, go visit The Crab Shack.

$$$ Challenge #3

➢ Do a wine tour and tasting at a local winery.

PLACE PICTURE HERE

PLACE PICTURE HERE

Culture & More Adventure

$ Challenge #1

➢ Experience the fluorescent rocks of Sterling Hill Mining Museum.

$$ Challenge #2

➢ Treat yourself to a fine dining experience and indulge in the scenery at Rat's Restaurant.

$$$ Challenge #3

➢ Visit Gardner's Basin and take a boat excursion or go fishing.

NEW MEXICO

TOP CITIES: Santa Fe, Albuquerque, Taos, Silver City, Los Alamos
BEST TIME TO TRAVEL: Summer (May–September)
SIGNATURE DRINKS: Margaritas, Chimayo Cocktail (tequila, crème de cassis, apple cider, fresh apples)
HIDDEN GEMS: Shiprock, Chaco Culture National Historical Park, Origami in the Garden, Bisti Badlands, Santa Fe Trail horseback riding, Ra Paulette art cave tour
BUCKET LIST: Bosque del Apache National Wildlife Refuge, Chaco Canyon, Kasha Katuwe Tent Rocks National Monument, Ah-Shi-Sle-Pah Wilderness
FESTIVALS: Albuquerque International Balloon Festival, New Mexico Burlesque Festival, Renaissance Celtic Festival, Donut Fest Albuquerque, Santa Fe Spanish Market, River of Lights holiday light display in Albuquerque

$Costs range from $35-$120

Activities

$ Challenge #1

- Go explore Lechuguilla Cave, the "most beautiful cave in the world" with 150 miles of passages.

$$ Challenge #2

- Relax in one of many natural hot springs in the city of Truth or Consequences. Fun fact, this small town is named after a television show.

$$$ Challenge #3

- Take the plunge into the Blue Hole of Santa Rosa. Diving or snorkeling, the choice is yours!

PLACE PICTURE HERE

NEW MEXICO

Food & Drinks

$ Challenge #1

> Eat like a local! Try some local food favorites: blue corn pancakes, Piñon Coffee, breakfast burrito, carne adovada, posole, green chile stew, chiles rellenos, frito pie, biscochito, sopaipillas, Indian tacos, green chile pizza, green chile cheeseburger, red cheese enchiladas, red chiles pork tamales, flame-roasted green chiles, green chile apple pie.

$$ Challenge #2

> Go day drinking at the best rooftop bar in the area and live in the moment.

$$$ Challenge #3

> Take a cooking class in Santa Fe and learn how to cook traditinal local dishes.

PLACE PICTURE HERE

PLACE PICTURE HERE

$Costs range from $25-$65

Culture & More Adventure

$ Challenge #1

> Hop on the Sandia Peak Tramway and take in the breathtaking mountain views.

$$ Challenge #2

> Go sleding or sink your feet into the dunes at White Sands National Park. Make it Instaworthy and put on your Sunday best for some fun, beautiful pictures.

$$$ Challenge #3

> Stand, sit, or lie in four states at a time at the Four Corners Monument. Don't forget to capture the moment!

NEW YORK

TOP CITIES: New York City, Albany, Manhattan, Buffalo, Brooklyn, Rochester, Queens, Bronx, Syracuse, Staten Island

BEST TIME TO TRAVEL: Spring (April-June), Winter (November-December)

SIGNATURE DRINKS: Long Island Iced Tea, Manhattan (bourbon, sweet vermouth, a dash of aromatic bitters, cherry)

HIDDEN GEMS: Lucifer Falls, Southwick Beach State Park, Camillus Erie Canal Park, Whitaker Park, Bannerman Castle on Pollepel Island, Hell's Kitchen Flea Market, Ellis Island, Roosevelt Island Aerial Tramway, New York Botanical Garden in the Bronx, Walk the High Line, Dead Horse Bay, IRT Lexington Avenue Line ghost stations

BUCKET LIST: Zoar Valley swimming hole, Whiteface Mountain steps, Watkins Glen State Park, Niagara Falls, Freedom Tunnel, Holiday Nostalgia Train, Smorgasburg Open Air Market, Statue of Liberty, Union Square Park, Rockefeller Center, Empire State Building, Central Park, One World Observatory Freedom Tower, Capture the world's best city skyline at night, Catch a play on Broadway, Attend a poetry reading in Greenwich Village, Guggenheim Museum

FESTIVALS: Tribeca Film Festival, NYC LGBT Pride Fest & March, Museum Mile Festival, River to River Festival, Celebrate Brooklyn, Bryant Park Film Festival, Rooftop Films, Fleet Week New York City, Street fairs and festivals, Harlem Week, BAM Next Wave Festival, CityParks Summer Stage, Afropunk Festival, Electric Zoo Festival

---

$Costs range from $75-$125

Activities

$ Challenge #1

➤ Visit the Chelsea Market and shop one-of-a-kind items created by a local artist. Tip: the meatpacking district location is a personal favorite.

$$ Challenge #2

➤ Cycle the Brooklyn Bridge to Manhattan. Don't forget to visit the "Love Locks" on the Brooklyn Bridge.

$$$ Challenge #3

➤ Pick One: Surf the Hudson River, Manhattan kayak skyline tour, Stand up paddle board yoga class, Jet ski the New York Harbor, or Row through Central Park via Loeb Boathouse.

PLACE PICTURE HERE

NEW YORK

$Costs range from $15-$35

Food & Drinks

$ Challenge #1

➢ Take a food tour and explore the best delis around New York.

$$ Challenge #2

➢ Eat like a local! Try some local food favorites: New York-style pizza, beef on wreck, black & white half moon cookie, chicken riggies, salt potatoes, New York cheesecake, Nathan's Famous Hot Dogs, spiedies, sponge candy, pastrami, a "BEC", falafel street meat.

$$$ Challenge #3

➢ Indulge your sweet tooth at Lexington Candy Shop.

PLACE PICTURE HERE

PLACE PICTURE HERE

$Costs range from $15-$40

Culture & More Adventure

$ Challenge #1

➢ Visit at least two of the museums that New York has to offer. Personal favorites: the Museum of Modern Art (MoMA), the Museum of Sex, the Metropolitan Museum of Art.

$$ Challenge #2

➢ Find the hidden Art Deco tunnel underneath The New Yorker Hotel. Don't stop there, do a self-guided street art tour. Bonus points if you visit the Storm King Art Center outdoor sculpture museum.

$$$ Challenge #3

➢ Ride the ferry from NYC to Staten Island.

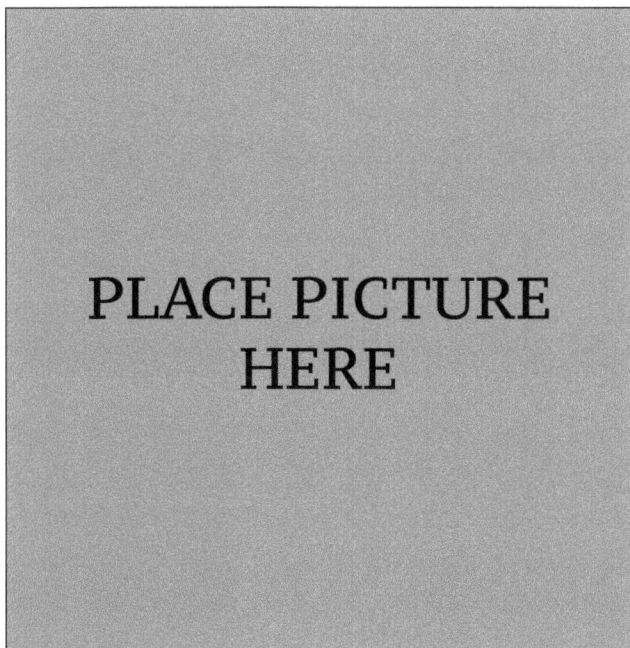

NORTH CAROLINA

TOP CITIES: Charlotte, Raleigh, Durham, Asheville, Wilmington, Winston-Salem
BEST TIME TO TRAVEL: Spring, Summer, Fall (March–August)
SIGNATURE DRINKS: Moonshine, Cherry Bounce (cherry vodka, cranberry juice, lime juice, club soda)
HIDDEN GEMS: Secret Falls, Jones Lake State Park, Cape Hatteras Light House
BUCKET LIST: Catawba Falls, The Great Smoky Mountains Railroad, Natural water slide in Bryson City, Go scuba diving at the historic shipwreck
FESTIVALS: Autumn Leaves Festival, Wilmington Riverfest, Carolina Renaissance Festival, Lexington BBQ Festival, Flicker Film Festival, Action Fest, Moogfest

$Costs range from $20-$65
Activities

$ Challenge #1

 ➢ Relax in a Treetop Soaking Cabana that overlooks Fontana Lake and the Smoky Mountains.

$$ Challenge #2

 ➢ Climb or hike Mount Mitchell to take in breathtaking views.

$$$ Challenge #3

 ➢ Feeling brave? Cross the Mile High Swinging Bridge, America's highest suspension footbridge, at Grandfather Mountain.

PLACE PICTURE HERE

NORTH CAROLINA

$Costs range from $20-$50

Food & Drinks

$ Challenge #1

➤ Eat like a local! Try some local food favorites: Lexington-style BBQ, fried green tomatoes, shrimp n' grits, Cheerwine float, she crab bisque, Moravian sugar cookies.

$$ Challenge #2

➤ Spend the day tasting wine on the Yadkin Valley Wine Trail.

$$$ Challenge #3

➤ Ask a local! Get a recommendation for a local resturant and the best dish to order.

PLACE PICTURE HERE

PLACE PICTURE HERE

$Costs range from $15-$45

Culture & More Adventure

$ Challenge #1

➤ Walk, rock climb, or bike to the top of Chimney Rock.

$$ Challenge #2

➤ Watch the sunset atop Jockey's Ridge, the tallest living sand dune on the Atlantic coast.

$$$ Challenge #3

➤ Take a day trip to the Outer Banks to watch the wild horses run along North Carolina's coast line.

NORTH DAKOTA

TOP CITIES: Fargo, Bismarck, Grand Forks, Minot
BEST TIME TO TRAVEL: Summer, Fall (May-October)
SIGNATURE DRINKS: Busch Lite, Chokecherry Bounce
HIDDEN GEMS: Chase Lake National Wildlife Refuge, Lewis and Clark State Park, Fort Ransom State Park, Section 9 Cyber Café, The Nekoma Pyramid
BUCKET LIST: Climb the highest point in the state at White Butte, Hotel Donaldson, Lund's Landing, Visit the Maah Daah Hey Trail and go Mountain Biking
FESTIVALS: Buggies-N-Blues, Ribfest, Fargo Film Festival, International Powwow in Bismarck

$Costs range from $20-$150

Activities

$ Challenge #1

➤ Bike through the majestic Japanese Gardens in Grand Forks.

$$ Challenge #2

➤ Explore Theodore Roosevelt National Park and take in 70,000 acres of painted canyons. Don't want to walk? Go on horseback!

$$$ Challenge #3

➤ Try your hand at ice fishing at Devils Lake, Lake Renwick in Icelandic State Park, Lake Metigoshe State Park, Lake Sakakawea, or Lake Audubon.

PLACE PICTURE HERE

NORTH DAKOTA

Food & Drinks

$ Challenge #1

> Eat like a local! Try some local food favorites: knoephla soup, walleye, fleischkuekle, Tater Tot hotdish, lefse, hot beef sandwich, goulash, cheese buttons/kase knoephla, kuchen, strawberry rhubarb pie, Chippers, taco in a bag, fry bread taco, bison steak.

$$ Challenge #2

> Treat yourself to a true one-of-a-kind culinary experience at Pitchfork Steak Fondue in Medora.

$$$ Challenge #3

> Ask a local! Get a recommendation for a local resturant, and don't forget to ask for the best dish to try.

PLACE PICTURE HERE

PLACE PICTURE HERE

$Costs range from $20-$175

Culture & More Adventure

$ Challenge #1

> Visit one of the following museums: National Buffalo Museum, Plains Art Museum, Paul Broste Rock Museum.

$$ Challenge #2

> Take a tour of the dam at Lake Sakakawea and Garrison Dam.

$$$ Challenge #3

> Instead of your typical accomodations, stay in an authentic earth lodge for a true cultural experience.

OHIO

TOP CITIES: Columbus, Cleveland, Cincinnati, Dayton, Toledo, Akron,
BEST TIME TO TRAVEL: Fall (September–October)
SIGNATURE DRINKS: Bloody Mary, Boozy Buckeye (hot chocolate, Baileys, bourbon, melted peanut butter, whipped cream), Buckeye Martini (gin, dry vermouth, black olives)
HIDDEN GEMS: Loveland Castle & Museum Château Laroche, Hartman Rock Garden, the Cincinnati Subway, Temple of Tolerance, Crystal Cove, Basket Building
BUCKET LIST: Cuyahoga Valley National Park, Brandywine Falls, Ohio State Reformatory, Put-In-Bay, Amish country, Go Ice Fishing on a Frozen Lake
FESTIVALS: Columbus Arts Festival, Bratwurst Festival Inc, Ohio Sauerkraut Festival, Ohio River Sternwheel Festival, Cincinnati International Wine Festival, Oxford Wine & Craft Beer Festival, Blue Tip Festival, BAYarts Art & Music Festival, Ohio Wings & Beer Festival, Cincinnati Music Festival

---

$Costs range from $35-$75

Activities

$ Challenge #1

➤ Grab the camera and visit the American Sign Museum.

$$ Challenge #2

➤ Enjoy a safari experience in the Wilds in Cumberland.

$$$ Challenge #3

➤ Take a ferry ride to one of the Lake Erie Islands.

PLACE PICTURE HERE

OHIO

$Costs range from $15-$65

Food & Drinks

$ Challenge #1

> Eat like a local! Try some local food favorites: buckeyes, Tony Packo's chili dogs, the Thurmanator, Syman's corned beef, Cleveland-style BBQ, Polish Boy, Hungarian hot dogs, goetta hash, paw paw wheat ale, bourbon barrel-aged maple syrup, NORKA Soda, sweet corn, fried late perch, Barberton-style chicken, pierogi.

$$ Challenge #2

> Try authentic German cuisine in the German Village of Columbus.

$$$ Challenge #3

> Hop aboard the Cuyahoga Valley Scenic Railroad for drinks and views that you will never forget.

PLACE PICTURE HERE

PLACE PICTURE HERE

$Costs range from $25-$175

Culture & More Adventure

$ Challenge #1

> Ever see a real-life castle? Make a trip to the allegedly haunted Squire's Castle in Willoughby Hills.

$$ Challenge #2

> Go caving! Explore Old Man's Cave or the Ohio Caverns.

$$$ Challenge #3

> Instead of staying in your typical accomodations, stay in a treehouse or a caboose!

OKLAHOMA

TOP CITIES: Oklahoma City, Tulsa, Norman, Lawton, Stillwater, Broken Arrow
BEST TIME TO TRAVEL: Fall (September-November)
SIGNATURE DRINKS: Lunchbox (beer, amaretto, and OJ), Boozy Strawberry Milkshake
HIDDEN GEMS: Pops Soda Ranch, Factory Obscura's Mix-Tape, Philbrook Museum of Art, Museum of Osteology
BUCKET LIST: Lake Heffner, Wichita Mountains Wildlife Refuge, Alabaster Caverns Sate Park, Visit Salt Plains National Wildlife Refuge and Dig to Find Your Own Crystals
FESTIVALS: Festival of Arts, OKC Pride Fest, Red Earth Festival, Plaza District Festival, Rocklahoma, Norman Music Festival, Poteau Balloon Festival

$Costs range from $15-$45

Activities

$ Challenge #1

➤ Visit Turner Falls which is the tallest waterfall in the state, sitting at 77 feet tall.

$$ Challenge #2

➤ Start your day off with a beautiful sunrise and hike to the top of Mt. Scott.

$$$ Challenge #3

➤ Grab the camera and spend the day at the Myriad Botanical Gardens & Crystal Bridge Tropical Conservatory.

PLACE PICTURE HERE

OKLAHOMA

Food & Drinks

$ Challenge #1

> Eat like a local! Try some local food favorites: barbecue, fried onion burger, chicken fried steak, fried pies, fried okra, calf fries, fried catfish, Sooner steaks, biscuits & sausage gravy, banh mi, Theta burger, pig sandwich.

$$ Challenge #2

> Visit one of the largest livestock markets in the world, the Historic Stockyards City.

$$$ Challenge #3

> Spend the day bar and resturant hopping in the Bricktown Entertainment District. Don't forget to hop on a water taxi on the canal!

PLACE PICTURE HERE

PLACE PICTURE HERE

Culture & More Adventure

$ Challenge #1

> Museum time! Check out one or more of the following: National Cowboy & Western Heritage Museum, Oklahoma City Museum of Art, Oklahoma City National Memorial & Museum

$$ Challenge #2

> Take a picture in front of these iconic landmarks in OKC: The Skydance Pedestrian Bridge, the Ferris wheel at Wheeler Park, and the Oklahoma city sign.

$$$ Challenge #3

> Go ATVing across the dunes in Little Sahara State Park.

OREGON

TOP CITIES: Portland, Salem, Eugene, Bend, Medford, Ashland, Astoria, Baker City
BEST TIME TO TRAVEL: Summer, Fall (July-August)
SIGNATURE DRINKS: Craft beer, Negroni (gin, sweet vermouth, Campari), Sloe Gin Fizz (Plymouth Sloe Gin, lemon juice, superfine sugar, club soda)
HIDDEN GEMS: Multnomah Falls in Portland, Canoe on Trillium Lake, Snowboard at Mount Hood, Snowshoe at Crater Lake, Sea Lion Caves, Airplane home in the woods, Lost Lake, No Name Lake, Oneonta Gorge, Enchanted Forest, Find the wishing tree in Portland and leave a wish, Ecola State Park, Powell's City of Books in Portland
BUCKET LIST: Drive across the Astoria-Megler Bridge, Smith Rock State Park, Hike South Sister, Toketee Falls, Samuel H Boardman State Scenic Corridor, Thor's Well, Explore tide pools on the coast, Washington Park, Go diving at Clear Lake, Go geocaching, Hop on a brewery bike tour in Portland
FESTIVALS: Oregon Jamboree, Waterfront Blues Fest, Sisters Folk Festival, PDX Pop Now!, Pendleton Whisky Music Fest, 4 Peaks Music Festival, Music Fest NW, Pendleton Round-Up, Wooden Shoe Tulip Festival, Christmas Festival of Lights at the Grotto

$Costs range from $60-$180

Activities

$ Challenge #1

➢ Go stand up paddle boarding on the turquoise waters of Devils Lake.

$$ Challenge #2

➢ Have a playful photoshoot at Oregon Sand Dunes National Park or the Painted Hills. Seeking more adventure? Hop on dune buggies and cruise the sandy terrain.

$$$ Challenge #3

➢ Do a horseback ride on the beach in Bandon.

PLACE PICTURE HERE

OREGON

$Costs range from $20-$45

Food & Drinks

$ Challenge #1

➤ Eat like a local! Try some local food favorites: Voodoo Doughnuts, Salt & Straw ice cream, Pok Pok's chicken wings, Tillamook cheese, Moonstruck chocolates, Dungeness crab, marionberries, pear & blue cheese ice cream, albacore tuna melt, hazelnuts, oysters.

$$ Challenge #2

➤ There are tons of unique bars and drinking experiences in Oregon. Search "unique bar experience" and visit the one that stands out to you the most.

$$$ Challenge #3

➤ Ask a local for dinner recommendations of a locally owned resertuant.

PLACE PICTURE HERE

PLACE PICTURE HERE

$Costs range from $15-$55

Culture & More Adventure

$ Challenge #1

➤ Hike Tamolitch Falls to see the Blue Pool.

$$ Challenge #2

➤ Visit Cannon Beach for a day to see Haystack Rock.

$$$ Challenge #3

➤ Take time to relax and soak in one of Oregon's natural hot springs. Visit www.TheTravelBella.com for recommendations.

PENNSYLVANIA

TOP CITIES: Philadelphia, Pittsburgh, Harrisburg, Scranton, Erie, Lancaster, Reading, Hershey
BEST TIME TO TRAVEL: Spring (March-May)
SIGNATURE DRINKS: Yuengling, Fish House Punch (sugar, lemon juice, black tea, rum, cognac, peach brandy, nutmeg garnish with lemon)
HIDDEN GEMS: Pinnacle Trail, Cherry Springs State Park, Pine Creek Gorge, Visit the Mural Arts, Ohiopyle State Park
BUCKET LIST: Niagara Falls, Mattress Factory in Pittsburgh, Seven Gates of Hell, Experience Amish country firsthand by riding an Amish horse-drawn buggy, spending a night on a working farm, or riding the Strasburg steam train
FESTIVALS: Elements Lakewood Music & Arts Festival, Camp Bisco, Big Dub Festival, Musik Fest, Made in America, Roots Picnic, Lady Fest, Three Rivers Arts Festival, Xponential Music Festival

$Costs range from $10-$40

Activities

$ Challenge #1

> Visit Philadelphia's Magic Gardens to take in the beautiful mosaic outdoor art labyrinth.

$$ Challenge #2

> Pack some light snacks and wine and watch the sunset at Presque Isle Park in Erie.

$$$ Challenge #3

> Spend the day at Penn's Landing waterfront and choose from various activities and restaurants to indulge in.

PLACE PICTURE HERE

PENNSYLVANIA

Food & Drinks

$ Challenge #1

➢ Eat like a local! Try some local food favorites: Philly cheesesteak, shoofly pie, whoopie pie, Tastykake, hoagies, birch beer, scrapple, Old Forge-style pizza, wedding soup, pierogies, burnt almond torte, snapper soup, Italian ice/water ice, roast port sandwich, Pittsburger, Pittsburgh salad.

$$ Challenge #2

➢ Battle of the Philly cheesesteaks! Find and try the two best Philly cheesesteak restaurants in town and pick a winner.

$$$ Challenge #3

➢ Go to the local produce market at the Lancaster Central Market to pick some fresh produce and enjoy the snacks.

PLACE PICTURE HERE

PLACE PICTURE HERE

$Costs range from $20-$65

Culture & More Adventure

$ Challenge #1

➢ Hop on the Duquesne Incline and take in the city views of Pittsburgh.

$$ Challenge #2

➢ Partake in a rare experience with a boat tour through Penn's Cave and try your luck with gemstone panning.

$$$ Challenge #3

➢ Go hiking and count how many waterfalls you are able to find on the Falls Trail System at Ricketts Glen State Park.

RHODE ISLAND

TOP CITIES: Providence, Newport, Warwick, Pawtucket, Cranston, Woonsocket, Bristol, Westerly, Narragansett, Portsmouth
BEST TIME TO TRAVEL: Spring (March–May), Fall (September-November)
SIGNATURE DRINKS: Dark and Stormy (black rum & ginger beer), Coffee Milk Cocktail (rum, Autocrat Coffee Syrup, milk, fresh nutmeg), Rhode Island Red (tequila, black raspberry liqueur, fresh squeezed lemon juice, agave syrup, a dash of orange bitters, top up with ginger beer)
HIDDEN GEMS: Sakonnet Garden, The Bells in Newport
BUCKET LIST: Point Judith, Brenton Point State Park, Kayak in Wickford, Sail Narragansett Bay
FESTIVALS: PrideFest, Federal Hill Summer Festival, Charlestown Seafood Festival, Newport Jazz Festival, FLICKERS Rhode Island International Film Festival, Rhythm & Roots Festival, Rhode Island Calamari Fest, Rhode Island Seafood Festival

---

$Costs range from $35-$125

Activities

$ Challenge #1

➢ Take a ferry ride to Block Island and explore on foot or by bike.

$$ Challenge #2

➢ Take a gondola ride while the water bonfires are burning during WaterFire Providence.

$$$ Challenge #3

➢ For a unique pedaling experience, take an adventurous but relaxing ride on the Rail Explorers located in Portsmouth.

PLACE PICTURE HERE

RHODE ISLAND

$Costs range from $20-$65

Food & Drinks

$ Challenge #1

➢ Eat like a local! Try some local food favorites: hot wieners, clam cakes, clam chowder, stuffies, fried clams, calamari, Del's Lemonade, lobster ravioli, zeppole, pizza strips, coffee cabinets, oysters, clams casino.

$$ Challenge #2

➢ Go on a scavenger hunt for the best food trucks in Providence.

$$$ Challenge #3

➢ For a unique culinary experience, vist the Fondue Village at the Ocean House.

PLACE PICTURE HERE

PLACE PICTURE HERE

$Costs range from $15-$40

Culture & More Adventure

$ Challenge #1

➢ Visit as many museums as you can: Newport Car Museum, Rough Point Museum, Newport Art Museum, National Museum of American Illustration.

$$ Challenge #2

➢ Surf at the Mohegan Bluffs or enjoy other beach activities.

$$$ Challenge #3

➢ Take an evening stroll on the Newport Cliffs and soak up views of the ocean, mansions, and nature.

SOUTH CAROLINA

TOP CITIES: Charleston, Columbia, Greenville, Myrtle Beach, Clemson. Spartanburg, Hilton Head

BEST TIME TO TRAVEL: Spring, Summer (March-July)

SIGNATURE DRINKS: Firefly Sweet Tea Vodka, Gin Fizz (gin, fresh lemon juice, simple syrup, egg white, club soda), Mint Julep

HIDDEN GEMS: Cypress Gardens, Lee Falls, Finlay Park, Rainbow Falls, Waterfront porch swings at Henry C. Chambers Waterfront Park, Oyotunji African Village, Mitchelville

BUCKET LIST: Caesars Head State Park, The Battery seawall & promenade, Sunset horseback ride on the beach, Shop at the historic Charleston City Market

FESTIVALS: Charleston Wine & Food Festival, Head Island Seafood Festival, South Carolina Festival of Flowers, Gullah Festival, Beaufort Water Festival, Greek Festival, Into the Woods Festival, Bourbon & Bacon Fest, MOJA Arts Festival

---

$Costs range from $25-$350

Activities

$ Challenge #1

➤ Visit White Point Gardens for great views of Charleston Harbor and Fort Sumter.

$$ Challenge #2

➤ Guide your own motorized creek cat boat to access small marshes and wildlife-rich areas on Hilton Head island.

$$$ Challenge #3

➤ It's time to splurge! Book a private charter on a sailboat and conquer the sea. Want to take the more economical route? Find a shared sailed boat tour.

PLACE PICTURE HERE

SOUTH CAROLINA

Food & Drinks

$ Challenge #1

➤ Eat like a local! Try some local food favorites: shrimp & grits, fatback, Southern sweet tea, cornbread, boiled peanuts, barbeque, she crab soup, biscuits, deviled eggs, peaches, fried seafood, oysters, pecans, meat and three, collards, okra, pimento cheese, Blenheim Ginger Ale, Carolina gold rice & fried fish, chow chow, Beaufort stew.

$$ Challenge #2

➤ Go on the hunt for some local souvenirs: Charleston Bloody Mary Mix, Benford Southern Tater Sweet Potato Ale.

$$$ Challenge #3

➤ Look up the best rated food tour in South Carolina and see what all the hype is about.

PLACE PICTURE HERE

PLACE PICTURE HERE

$Costs range from $20-$125

Culture & More Adventure

$ Challenge #1

➤ Visit Angel Oak of St. John's Island to see one of the oldest living trees in North America.

$$ Challenge #2

➤ Visit the iconic Tunnel Vision Mural in Columbia, South Carolina and try to capture some epic pictures.

$$$ Challenge #3

➤ Rent a scooter and do a self-guided tour around town.

SOUTH DAKOTA

TOP CITIES: Sioux Falls, Pierre, Rapid City, Deadwood, Keystone
BEST TIME TO TRAVEL: Summer (June–August)
SIGNATURE DRINKS: Red Beer (beer, tomato juice, olives), South Dakota Martini (Red Beer with a pickle stuck in it), The Roosevelt (dark rum, dry vermouth, fresh OJ, sugar)
HIDDEN GEMS: Palisades State Park, Pactola Lake, Sylvan Lake
BUCKET LIST: Mount Rushmore National Monument, Black Elk Peak, Crazy Horse Memorial, Buffalo watching at Custer State Park
FESTIVALS: Sturgis Motorcycle Rally, JazzFest Sioux Falls, 1880 Train Oktoberfest Express, State Fair in Huron

$Costs range from $25-$325

Activities

$ Challenge #1

➢ With layers of rock formations, prairie dogs, bison, and bighorn sheep, Badlands National Park is a trip to remember.

$$ Challenge #2

➢ Hike or bike the Mickelson Mountain Trail.

$$$ Challenge #3

➢ Take a hot air balloon ride over the Black Hills.

PLACE PICTURE HERE

SOUTH DAKOTA

$Costs range from $12-$30

Food & Drinks

$ Challenge #1

➤ Eat like a local! Try some local food favorites: Indian tacos, bierocks, pheasant, walleye, chislic, kuchen, Dimock Dairy cheese, Rocky Mountain oysters, kolache, lefse, rhubarb, fleisch kuchele, wojapi, Indian fry bread, buffalo, Zebra donuts, tiger meat, mocha cakes.

$$ Challenge #2

➤ Take a food tour in downtown Sioux Falls.

$$$ Challenge #3

➤ Want to try some of the best macaroons? Start the hunt now! Ask locals and look online for the best of the best.

PLACE PICTURE HERE

PLACE PICTURE HERE

$Costs range from $10-$99

Culture & More Adventure

$ Challenge #1

➤ Pick a museum and go: Redline Art Center, National Music Museum, South Dakota Air and Space Museum, Old Courthouse Museum.

$$ Challenge #2

➤ Do ziplining and other aerial adventures in Keystone near Mt. Rushmore.

$$$ Challenge #3

➤ Take some creative pictures with the graffiti art and murals in Art Alley, Rapid City.

TENNESSEE

TOP CITIES: Nashville, Memphis, Knoxville, Chattanooga, Manchester, Gatlinburg, Pigeon Forge, Bristol
BEST TIME TO TRAVEL: Summer, Winter (July-January)
SIGNATURE DRINKS: Jack & Coke, Lynchburg Lemonade (Jack Daniels, triple sec, sour mix, lime, lemon), Moonshine
HIDDEN GEMS: Rock Island State Park, Burgess Falls State Park, Hurricane Mills, Moonshine Distillery
BUCKET LIST: Hike the Smoky Mountains, Visit the National Civil Rights Museum Lorraine Motel
FESTIVALS: Bonnaroo Music and Arts Festival, Bloomin' Barbeque & Bluegrass Festival, Live On The Green, Wine Over Water Festival, Southern Hot Wing Festival, CMA Music Festival, Riverbend Festival, Memphis Comedy Festival

$Costs range from $25-$99

Activities

$ Challenge #1

➢ Stroll to Lover's Leap at the top of Lookout Mountain where you'll be able to see 7 states from atop a 100-foot waterfall.

$$ Challenge #2

➢ Spend the day at Big South Fork National River and Recreation Area. Pack a picnic and enjoy some paddling, rock climbing, hiking, or fishing.

$$$ Challenge #3

➢ Hop on the Dollywood Express Steam Train for the most scenic journey through the Smoky Mountains.

PLACE PICTURE HERE

TENNESSEE

$Costs range from $15-$85

Food & Drinks

$ Challenge #1

➤ Eat like a local! Try some local food favorites: fried pickles, catfish, barbecue, mac n' cheese, country ham, banana pudding, hot fried chicken, dry ribs, Goo Goo Clusters, cornbread, meat and three, greens and potlikker, Bushwacker, hot fish sandwich, moon pie, BBQ spaghetti, vinegar pie.

$$ Challenge #2

➤ Ask a local! Get a recommendation for the best BBQ restaurant in town.

$$$ Challenge #3

➤ Take a tour of the Jack Daniels Distillery. Don't forget to leave with a personalized bottle!

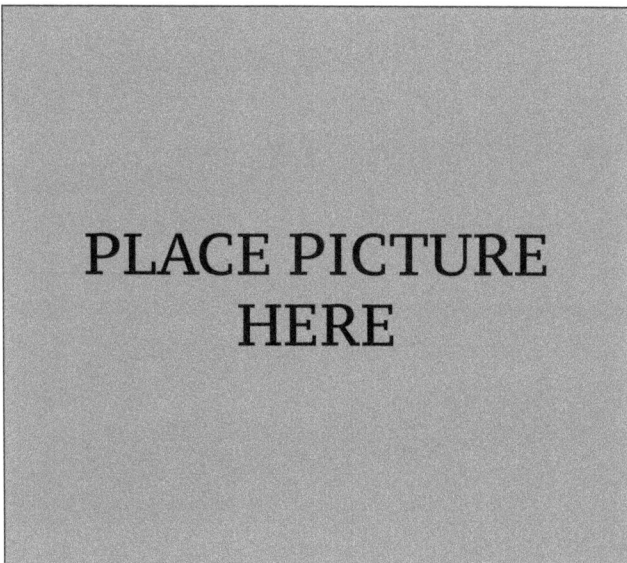

PLACE PICTURE HERE

PLACE PICTURE HERE

$Costs range from $10-$45

Culture & More Adventure

$ Challenge #1

➤ Soak up some culture at the National Museum of African American Music.

$$ Challenge #2

➤ Take a stroll on the Memphis River Walk and eat, drink, and shop until you drop.

$$$ Challenge #3

➤ It's time to party! Head to Beale Street for a night of fun, drinks, eats, and good beats!

TEXAS

TOP CITIES: Houston, Austin, San Antonio, Dallas, El Paso, Fort Worth, Amarillo, Galveston
BEST TIME TO TRAVEL: Spring, Summer (March-August)
SIGNATURE DRINKS: Shiner Bock, Paloma (red grapefruit juice, tequila), Fresh Margarita
HIDDEN GEMS: Prada Marfa, VW Slug Bug Ranch, Ozymandias on the Plains
BUCKET LIST: Big Bend National Park, San Antonio River Walk, Go Kiteboarding on South Parde Island
FESTIVALS: South by Southwest, Austin City Limits Music Festival, Levitation, UTOPIAfest, River City Rockfest

$Costs range from $15-$55

Activities

$ Challenge #1

➢ Take a dip in the waterfall spilling over the top of a limestone rock formation at the beautiful Hamilton Pool Preserve.

$$ Challenge #2

➢ It's photoshoot time! Put on your best couture and head to Cadillac Ranch In Amarillo for a day of fun pics.

$$$ Challenge #3

➢ Head to the beach for some fun in the sun at Padre Island National Seashore. Try parasailing or other beach activities.

PLACE PICTURE HERE

TEXAS

Food & Drinks

$ Challenge #1

> Eat like a local! Try some local food favorites: barbeque, chili, kolaches, Tex-Mex shredded beef sandwich, white Texas sheet cake, tacos al pastor, chili con queso, maple-glazed donuts, brisket, enchiladas, puffy taco, beef ribs, Gulf oysters, breakfast taco.

$$ Challenge #2

> Go bar hopping to find out who makes the best fresh Margaritas from scratch.

$$$ Challenge #3

> Ask a local! Find the best local taco joint.

PLACE PICTURE HERE

PLACE PICTURE HERE

Culture & More Adventure

$ Challenge #1

> Stroll down the beautiful flower-lined paths of the Shangri La Botanical Gardens in Orange.

$$ Challenge #2

> Go swimming in Jacob's Well artesian spring near Wimberley.

$$$ Challenge #3

> Enjoy the whimsical feel of the colors and art of Umbrella Alley, Baytown.

UTAH

TOP CITIES: Salt Lake City, Provo, St. George, Ogden, Park City, Moab, Deer Valley
BEST TIME TO TRAVEL: Spring, Late Fall, Winter (April-May, September-December)
SIGNATURE DRINKS: Root beer, Utah Salt (genever, lime, chamomile syrup, Génépy des Alpes, Real Salt rim), Polygamy Nitro Porter
HIDDEN GEMS: Nine Mile Canyon, Sun Tunnels, Capital Reef National Park, Canyonlands National Park, Arches National Park, Mount Timpanogos, Summum Pyramid
BUCKET LIST: Snowmobiling, skiing and sleigh riding in the Winter, Hike Calf Creek Falls, Fly fishing in the Provo River, Canyoneering at Zion National Park, 4x4 Burr Trail, Discover slot canyons, Float in the Great Salt Lake, Visit a Slot Canyon and Take Some Fun Pictures
FESTIVALS: Sundance Film Festival, Utah Arts Festival, Tulip Festival at Thanksgiving Point, Moab Music Festival, Deer Valley Music Festival

---

$Costs range from $20-$85

Activities

$ Challenge #1

➢ Go star gazing amongst the hoodoos at Bryce Canyon with a ranger program, special event or a self-guided tour to get spectacular views of the Milky Way.

$$ Challenge #2

➢ Visit the Mystic Hot Springs or the free Meadow Hot Springs for a day of relaxation and nature.

$$$ Challenge #3

➢ Spend the day at the world-famous Lake Powell. Want to make it super epic? Go paddle boarding or houseboating through winding bays and canyons with arches, hoodoos, and more!

PLACE PICTURE HERE

UTAH

$Costs range from $15-$65

Food & Drinks

$ Challenge #1

➢ Eat like a local! Try some local food favorites: Utah scones, Fernwood mint sandwiches, pastrami burgers, Dutch oven dinners, fry sauce, funeral potatoes, Navajo tacos, Utah corn, wild game chili.

$$ Challenge #2

➢ Find a rooftop bar and go day drinking. Visit www.TheTravelBella.com for recommendations.

$$$ Challenge #3

➢ Vist the High West distillery to sample Spicy Homemade Lemondae, Double Rye Whiskey, and more.

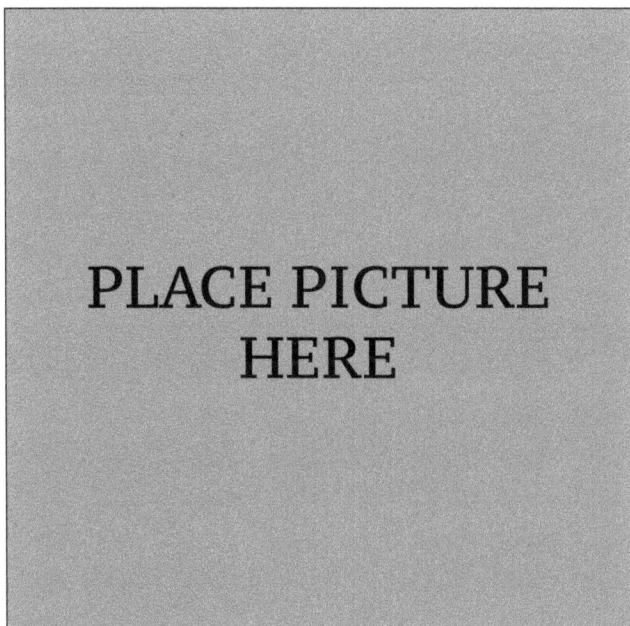

PLACE PICTURE HERE

PLACE PICTURE HERE

$Costs range from $5-$235

Culture & More Adventure

$ Challenge #1

➢ Put on your best water-resistant boots and explore the Narrows in Zion.

$$ Challenge #2

➢ Go sailing on the Great Salt Lake.

$$$ Challenge #3

➢ For a one-of-a-kind experience, go bobsledding at the Olympic Park.

VERMONT

TOP CITIES: Burlington, Montpelier, Killington, Rutland
BEST TIME TO TRAVEL: Spring, Summer, Fall (April–November)
SIGNATURE DRINKS: Craft beer, Old Vermont (gin, grade B pure maple syrup, lemon juice, a dash of bitters)
HIDDEN GEMS: Shelburne Museum, Robert Hull Fleming Museum of Art, Ski the 300-mile Catamount Trail, Brattleboro Area Farmers' Market, American Museum of Fly Fishing
BUCKET LIST: Hike Mt. Philo for panoramic views, Buy maple syrup souvenirs
FESTIVALS: Strolling of the Heifers parade and festival, Discover Jazz Festival, Quechee Hot Air Balloon Craft and Music Festival, Festival of Fools, Vermont Cheesemakers' Festival

$Costs range from $25-$75

Activities

$ Challenge #1

➢ Skate the 4.5-mile loop on Lake Morey, the longest outdoor skating track in the U.S.

$$ Challenge #2

➢ Hike or climb to the highest peak in Vermont at Mt. Mansfield.

$$$ Challenge #3

➢ Catch an hour-long ferry ride across Lake Champlain from Vermont to New York and enjoy spectacular views.

PLACE PICTURE HERE

VERMONT

$Costs range from $15-$45

Food & Drinks

$ Challenge #1

- Eat like a local! Try some local food favorites: apple pie cheddar, fiddleheads, maple cream, lamb, bison burger, venison, cider donuts, sugar on snow, strawberry rhubarb pie, chicken pot pie, aged cheddar, chili dogs, lake perch, gravy fries, switchel, maple cream pie, ramps, Gilfeather turnip, pickled eggs, maple baked beans, tourtiere, heirloom corn, spring dug parsnips, skinny.

$$ Challenge #2

- Tour the Ben & Jerry's factory. Don't forget to visit the flavor graveyard to see where the retired flavors are laid to rest!

$$$ Challenge #3

- Ask a local! Get recommendations for the best local restaurant and the best dish to order.

PLACE PICTURE HERE

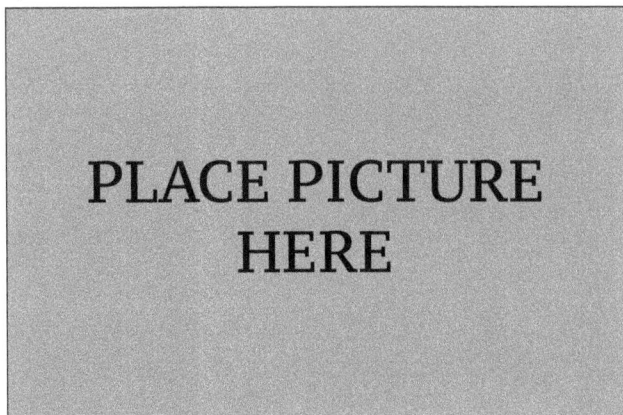

PLACE PICTURE HERE

$Costs range from $20-$55

Culture & More Adventure

$ Challenge #1

- Check out the Billings Farm & Museum Jersey dairy farm.

$$ Challenge #2

- Make your own chocolate bar at Lake Champlain Chocolates.

$$$ Challenge #3

- Complete all four tasks: Find three murals and take selfies, Swim and do waterfront yoga at North Beach, Go cheese tasting on the Vermont Cheese Trail, and try blueberry wine at Charlotte Village winery.

VIRGINIA

TOP CITIES: Richmond, Virginia Beach, Norfolk, Alexandria, Charlottesville, Roanoke, Jamestown, Williamsburg, Chesapeake, Hampton, Newport News
BEST TIME TO TRAVEL: Summer, Fall (May-October)
SIGNATURE DRINKS: Orange Crush, Appalachian Manhattan (whiskey, vermouth, bitters), Gin Rickey (gin, lime juice, soda water), Virginia wine
HIDDEN GEMS: President Heads, Dinosaurland, Virginia's Natural Tunnel, Savage Neck Dunes, Great Dismal Swamp
BUCKET LIST: Hike Mt. Rogers, Great Falls Park, Swim at Panther Falls natural pools, Climb to the top of Birch Knob Tower, Paddle or float on the James River
FESTIVALS: Norfolk festivals, Virginia Highlands Festival, PANorama Caribbean Music Fest, Old Fiddlers' Convention, Ella Fitzgerald Music Festival, Richmond Folk Festival, American Music Festival, Richmond Jazz and Music Festival, Virginia Film Festival, Rooster Walk Music & Arts Festival, Red Wing Roots Music Festival

---

$Costs range from $25-$135

Activities

$ Challenge #1

> Grab a tent and go beach camping at False Cape State Park.

$$ Challenge #2

> Rent a car and take the scenic, 105-mile Skyline Drive through the Blue Ridge Mountains in Shenandoah National Park.

$$$ Challenge #3

> Take a sunset dolphin kayak tour alongside the historic Cape Henry in Virginia Beach.

PLACE PICTURE HERE

VIRGINIA

$Costs range from $15-$45

Food & Drinks

$ Challenge #1

> Eat like a local! Try some local food favorites: Virginia crab cake, peach cobbler, Brunswick stew, Chesapeake Bay crab, homegrown peanuts, Rappahannock oysters, peanut pie, apple butter, baked oysters, stone ground pancakes, ham biscuits, barbeque, fried pies, trout, soft shell crab, peanut soup, shad roe.

$$ Challenge #2

> Paint the town and check out the night life on the waterfront in Old Town Alexandria.

$$$ Challenge #3

> Skip the typical night out and find a speakeasy (Richmond) or a traditional tea room (Virginia Beach).

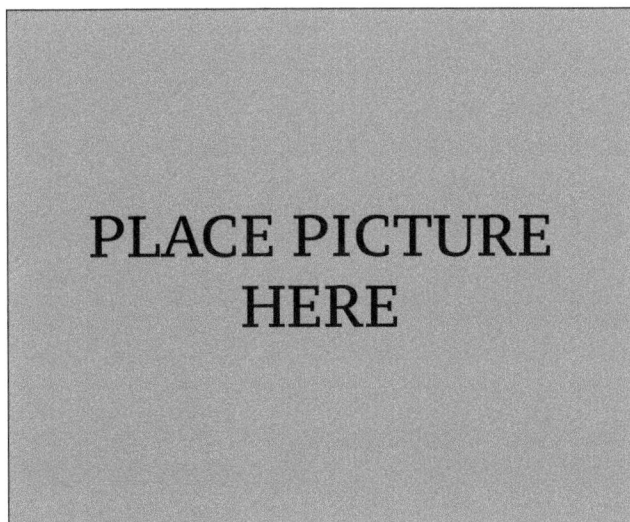

PLACE PICTURE HERE

PLACE PICTURE HERE

$Costs range from $25-$60

Culture & More Adventure

$ Challenge #1

> Explore and discover the Luray Caverns. Don't forget to make a wish while you are there!

$$ Challenge #2

> Stop horsing around! Wake up early and head to Assateague Island and watch the wild horses run free at sunrise.

$$$ Challenge #3

> Go geocaching and stargazing at Staunton River State Park.

WASHINGTON

TOP CITIES: Seattle, Olympia, Spokane, Tacoma, Vancouver, Bellevue
BEST TIME TO TRAVEL: Summer, Fall (June-August)
SIGNATURE DRINKS: Rainier beer, Washington Apple (whiskey, sour apple schnapps, cranberry juice), Rickey (gin or bourbon, fresh squeezed lime, seltzer water)
HIDDEN GEMS: Skagit Valley tulip fields (April), Hobbit House, Bridge of Glass, Mount St. Helens, Mount Rainier Scenic Railroad train
BUCKET LIST: Hike Palouse Falls, Lake Diablo, Lake Chelan, Seek out the Fremont Troll in Seattle
FESTIVALS: Beyond Wonderland, Lucky Festival, Summer Meltdown Festival, Bumbershoot Festival, Watershed Music Festival, Seattle Hempfest Protestival, Volume Inlander Music Festival, Above & Beyond Group Therapy Weekender

---

$Costs range from $35-$150

Activities

$ Challenge #1

➢ Go camping on Shi Shi Beach in Olympic National Park.

$$ Challenge #2

➢ Go backpacking in 'Instaworthy' Enchantment Lakes, the crown jewel of hiking in Washington.

$$$ Challenge #3

➢ Hop on the ferry to the San Juan Islands for world-class whale watching. You can hop on a kayak or sea plane to make the experience even more unique. Afterwards you can visit a lavender farm or Island hop to Orcas Island, Lopez Island, and Lummi Island.

PLACE PICTURE HERE

WASHINGTON

Food & Drinks

$ Challenge #1

> Eat like a local! Try some local food favorites: smoked sockeye salmon, sauteed geoduck, oysters on the half shell, oyster stew, Beecher's "World's Best" Mac & Cheese, steamed mussels & clams, razor clam chowder, geoduck crudo, salmon sandwich, morels on toast, Saigon-style Dungeness crab, Dungeness crab roll, honey lavender ice cream, fish & chips, Aplets & Cotlets, Almond Roca.

$$ Challenge #2

> Create your own self-guided food tour. Need help with planning? Visit TheTravelBella.com for a Foodie Guide.

$$$ Challenge #3

> Known to have one of the largest collections of spirits in the Western Hemisphere, go on a treasure hunt for this bar and try some adventurous cocktails!

PLACE PICTURE HERE

PLACE PICTURE HERE

Culture & More Adventure

$ Challenge #1

> Hang out at Olympic National Park. Don't forget to hunt for the Tree of Life during low tide.

$$ Challenge #2

> Visit Ruby Beach for the incredible scenery of sea stacks and tide pools. This natural beauty will have you feeling like a kid again. Climb rocks while getting your feet wet!

$$$ Challenge #3

> Skip the traditional accomodations and stay at one of the renown mountain huts for a night or two.

WEST VIRGINIA

TOP CITIES: Charleston, Morgantown, Huntington, Harpers Ferry
BEST TIME TO TRAVEL: Spring to Fall (May-August)
SIGNATURE DRINK: Moonshine, Gin & Tonic, Copperhead (vodka, ginger ale, lime)
HIDDEN GEMS: Climb the Via Ferrata Telluride, Bike, Ski or snowboard at Snowshoe Mountain
BUCKET LIST: Whitewater rafting or ziplining in New River Gorge, Get up close and personal with falcons
FESTIVALS: Wanderlust Festival, Mountain Music Festival, 4848 Festival, DomeFest, All Good Music Festival, The Country Fest

---

$Costs range from $15-$150

Activities

$ Challenge #1

➢ Walk the catwalk below the New River George Bridge or walk across the 900 ft bridge if you are daring.

$$ Challenge #2

➢ Spend the day exploring all that Harpers Ferry National Historical Park has to offer.

$$$ Challenge #3

➢ Go ATVing on the Hatfield-McCoy Trails.

PLACE PICTURE HERE

WEST VIRGINIA

$Costs range from $15-$80

Food & Drinks

$ Challenge #1

> Eat like a local! Try some local food favorites: pepperoni rolls, chili & slaw dogs, cornbread & pinto beans, venison, spaghetti & meatballs, Mexican cornbread, potato cake, biscuits & gravy, grape & gorgonzola pizza, apple dumplings, buckwheat pancakes, Mountaineer Biscuit, pot roast melt, wild game, double-cut pork chop, West Virginia dog

$$ Challenge #2

> Head to The Winery (Robert F. Pliska & Company Winery) to taste wine and stomp grapes.

$$$ Challenge #3

> Ask a local! Get dinner recommendations for a locally owned resertuant.

PLACE PICTURE HERE

PLACE PICTURE HERE

$Costs range from $5-$300

Culture & More Adventure

$ Challenge #1

> Hike the Endless Wall Trail and snap an Instaworthy picture at the top!

$$ Challenge #2

> Go climbing at Seneca Rocks.

$$$ Challenge #3

> Ride into yesterday on the Cass Scenic Railroad steam train. Treat yourself to a snack or souvenir!

WISCONSIN

TOP CITIES: Milwaukee, Madison, Green Bay, Racine, Appleton, La Crosse
BEST TIME TO TRAVEL: Summer (June-August)
SIGNATURE DRINK: Brandy Old Fashioned
HIDDEN GEMS: Mirror Lake State Park, Lake Geneva, Pewits Nest State Area, Devil's Lake State Park
BUCKET LIST: High Cliff State Park, Paddle the Wisconsin River, Schoolhouse Beach, Ski through the Birkebeiner Trail System
FESTIVALS: Porterfield Country Music Festival, Summerfest, Sugar Maple Music Festival, Harbor Park Jazz Rhythm & Blues Festival

$Costs range from $25-$250

Activities

$ Challenge #1

➤ Take a horse-drawn carriage ride through the Lost Canyons.

$$ Challenge #2

➤ Visit the natural wonder of Cave Point by bike, kayak, or on foot.

$$$ Challenge #3

➤ Explore the Apostle Islands by boat.

PLACE PICTURE HERE

WISCONSIN

$Costs range from $15-$30

Food & Drinks

$ Challenge #1

➤ Eat like a local! Try some local food favorites: bratwurst, cream puffs, roesti/rosti, Limburger sandwich, Swedish pancakes, Danish kringle, beer cheese soup, fried cheese curds, Colby cheese, artisanal cheese plate, fish boil, frozen custard, Hmong's Golden Egg Rolls, Cornish pasties, butter burgers, smoked fish chowder, chicken booyah.

$$ Challenge #2

➤ Spend the day at a cheese factory to see how it is all made. Don't forget to sample them!

$$$ Challenge #3

➤ Dine at the renown Ishnala Supper Club. Be sure to try their signature cocktails.

PLACE PICTURE HERE

PLACE PICTURE HERE

$Costs range from $25-$110

Culture & More Adventure

$ Challenge #1

➤ Go fishing at Big Manitou Falls.

$$ Challenge #2

➤ Take a stroll on the Wisconsin Dells Riverwalk.

$$$ Challenge #3

➤ Spend the day at the Historic Third Ward in Milwaukee for a day of art, food, drinks and shopping.

WYOMING

TOP CITIES: Jackson Hole, Cheyenne, Casper, Laramie, Rock Springs
BEST TIME TO TRAVEL: Winter (October to late March)
SIGNATURE DRINK: Wyoming Whiskey (whiskey, Galliano, egg, honey, orange juice, ginger), The Grizzly Bear (amaretto, Jägermeister, Kahlua, milk), Broiler Maker
HIDDEN GEMS: Big Spring, Grand Teton National Park
BUCKET LIST: Horseback riding, Skiing, Rafting at Snake River, Fly fishing, Take a Safari Ride through the Wild at Grand Teton National Park
FESTIVALS: Wyoming Brewers Festival, Cody Ice Climbing Festival, Jackson Hole Rendezvous Festival

$Costs range from $35-$120

Activities

Challenge #1

➢ Select any one of these great locations and go fly fishing: Snake River, Green River, North Plate River, Yellowstone River.

Challenge #2

➢ You don't have to visit Iceland to see amazing geysers! Visit the Grand Prismatic Spring in Yellowstone National Park and be amazed.

Challenge #3

➢ Feeling daring? Climb Devils Tower and learn its history.

PLACE PICTURE HERE

WYOMING

$Costs range from $15-$40

Food & Drinks

Challenge #1

> Eat like a local! Try some local food favorites: bison steak, chicken fried steak, buffalo chili, elk burger, cutthroat trout, fresh jerky, fry bread, Rocky Mountain oysters, lamb, soda bread, Wyomatoes, Sloshies, cowboy cookies

Challenge #2

> Visit the famous Million Dollar Cowboy Bar. Have a seat at the bar on the iconic saddle bar stools!

Challenge #3

> Research the best restaurants in the area and create your own self-guided food tour. If you don't care to do your own research, visit www.TheTravelBella.com for a Foodie Guide.

PLACE PICTURE HERE

PLACE PICTURE HERE

$Costs range from $75-$275

Culture & More Adventure

Challenge #1

> For the best views in town, take a ride on the Aerial Tram at Jackson Hole Mountain.

Challenge #2

> Just let it all go and live a little! For the ultimate adventure, learn paragliding or take a tandem flight!

Challenge #3

> Partake in the ultimate winter wonderland experience: snowmobiling in Yellowstone National Park.

Don't miss out on any future announcements. Follow us on all of our social platforms

Instagram: TheRealTravelBella

Facebook: The Travel Bella

YouTube: The Travel Bella

Pinterest: The Travel Bella

TikTok: The Travel Bella

Don't forget to visit our website: www.TheTravelBella.com

Coming Soon!

The Adventure Travelers Guide : Aruba Edition

www.ingramcontent.com/pod-product-compliance
Lightning Source LLC
Chambersburg PA
CBHW062009150426
42812CB00013BA/2587